Planning and Organizing Business Reports

Planning and Organizing Business Reports

Written, Oral, and Research-Based

Dorinda Clippinger

BEP BUSINESS EXPERT PRESS

Planning and Organizing Business Reports: Written, Oral, and Research-Based

First published in 2016 by
Business Expert Press, LLC
222 East 46th Street, New York, NY 10017
www.businessexpertpress.com

ISBN-13: 978-1-63157-413-9 (paperback)
ISBN-13: 978-1-63157-414-6 (e-book)

Business Expert Press Corporate Communication Collection

Collection ISSN: 2156-8162 (print)
Collection ISSN: 2156-8170 (electronic)

Cover and interior design by Exeter Premedia Services Private Ltd., Chennai, India

First edition: 2016

10 9 8 7 6 5 4 3 2 1

Printed in the United States of America.

Abstract

Planning and Organizing Business Reports: Written, Oral, and Research-Based emphasizes the importance of planning reports to ensure they do what you, as the writer or presenter, want them to do. This book is for you if you are

- A business manager or other professional who must convey objective, organized information to others, in and outside your organization.
- An MBA candidate or an upper-level student in any professional field.

The following list suggests some of the book's content:

- Describes and shows attributes that make reports effective.
- Gives pointers for writing to people who read English as a second (or third) language.
- Provides the steps in planning both a written report and an oral report (presentation) by individuals and teams.
- Examines models for ethical reporting.
- Highlights both ineffective and effective examples of writing and presenting.
- Gives special information about presentation slides and handouts.
- Includes tips for preparing online presentations (webinars).
- Offers ways to structure and outline report information.
- Shows the steps in planning business research and preparing a research proposal.
- Refers to numerous websites for finding even more information on specific topics.

Numerous examples, helpful illustrations, and a concise writing style let you acquire vital information rapidly, and each chapter ends with a convenient checklist. In *Planning and Organizing Business Reports* you

have a how-to guide for the various types of reports you generate throughout your career!

Keywords

audience, business, characteristics, delivery, guides, identify, organizing,
outlining, planning, presentation, purpose, reports, research, structure,
style

Contents

Preface

Planning and Organizing Business Reports: Written, Oral, and Research-Based is designed to help business managers, MBA candidates, and upper-level college students develop business reporting skills. Think of reports as organized, objective presentations of facts, experiences, or observations used in the decision-making process. Some reports are short, simple e-mails; others are much longer and more complex. This book is the ideal tool for mastering all kinds.

While the market is inundated with books on written and oral reports, none emphasizes the analytical process of reporting to the extent this book does. The words analytical process may make you wonder if the book deals in abstractions. Be assured, the book gives many, many concrete examples showing how the process works.

The main purpose of *Planning and Organizing Business Reports* is to enable readers to approach their reporting responsibilities with confidence. Guides in this book emphasize the planning and structuring of written and oral reports when working individually or collaboratively with team members. The guides also aim to increase efficiency and effectiveness in research and reporting by taking advantage of current technologies and practicing sound business ethics.

In the book's three chapters, readers are led through the essentials of planning and organizing business reports. The content is summarized as follows:

- Chapter 1 defines business reports and discusses and illustrates the characteristics of effective business reports. This chapter includes guides for reporting to people for whom English is a second language. Guides to ethical reporting are also included here.
- Chapter 2 guides readers in planning, organizing, and outlining written reports and presentations. It helps readers

understand and implement appropriate writing and presentation delivery styles. Guides include slide decks and audience handouts.

- Chapter 3 focuses on techniques for planning business research. Guides include writing a research proposal (models provided) and choosing sources of research data.

Planning and Organizing Business Reports: Written, Oral, and Research-Based provides instruction in planning effective business reports as ethical individuals working in a collaborative, high-tech, and global business environment.

Acknowledgments

I am indebted to Dr. Shirley Kuiper, who laid the foundation for this publication decades ago. And I am grateful to Dr. Debbie DuFrene, the expert editor who transformed a draft into a truly reader-friendly book. Thanks, also, to my husband, William Jewell, for his unfailing support. During my half century of teaching, publishing, research, and business ownership, many students and colleagues influenced my thinking about communication and education for business. I owe a huge debt to them.

CHAPTER 1

Report Characteristics

What do a manager at Bank of America, a BestBuy.com manager, a broker for Unique Import Export Company of Houston, and an executive director of the nonprofit organization United Way have in common? Although their jobs involve widely different duties, one task is common to all: preparing reports.

The word report may remind you of your student days when you wrote term papers, book reviews, and case studies. But those documents differ from on-the-job reports in many respects. While students write term papers to demonstrate their knowledge of a subject, you will create business reports to influence the actions of other people. Although school reports usually flow upward (from student to instructor), business reports move up, down, and across the formal organizational structure and even across organizational boundaries. For a college term paper, you may have searched the Web and accessed books, databases, and periodicals in your school library. But your business reports will frequently contain data drawn from company files or your own experiences and observations, as well as from electronic and print media. While the quality of a term paper may have affected your grade, the quality of a business report can determine the success or failure of your career—and that of your company.

Such differences in writing characterize what is known as a genre: a distinctive type or category of composition. You are familiar with different music genres, such as classical, jazz, hip hop, and rock. Although some elements of music overlap those genres, each also has style elements and conventions that are unique, differentiating one genre from another. The same is true of writing genres. The writing style used in a critical essay, a lab report, or a poem usually is not effective in a business report. The business writing genre uses certain conventions not common to scientific or literary writing. Those conventions are based on the function that each report serves and require thoughtful analysis of the writer's or presenter's purpose and audience needs.

Functions of Business Reports

Business reports can be defined as organized, objective presentations of observations, experiences, or facts used in the decision-making process. To understand the functions of business reports, several words in the definition need further analysis: organized, objective, and decision-making process.

Business Reports Are Organized

To be organized, a report—whether in a written medium or oral—must be planned and presented with both the receiver's needs and the sender's objectives in mind. Effective report creators define the report objective in terms of desired action—what the sender wants the receiver to do. But to achieve that action, the sender must consider the receiver's needs—both information needs and ego needs. Information needs are met when the sender supplies facts and data the receiver needs for understanding and fulfillment. Ego needs are a person's desire for recognition and an acknowledgment of that person's worth to the organization. A report may provide all the information a person needs; but unless the report also satisfies ego needs, the receiver may have no motivation to act. Information needs and ego needs influence the structure of a report as well as its content.

Two basic strategies for most messages are the direct and the indirect structure. Direct structure simulates deductive reasoning, which moves from generalizations to specific examples or facts to support those generalizations. The following paragraph demonstrates direct structure.

In the redesign of our office space, the number of individual work spaces will be reduced, and each space will be shared by two employees. The amount of common work space will be increased and will be appropriately configured for both individual and collaborative work as well as client meetings.

Last year's 15% increase in office staff has required us to examine the efficiency or our space usage. Since many employees already tele-commute as many as three days a week, approximately 60% of our desks are vacant at one time. Instead of renting additional office space, we will be redesigning the current office space with the goal of reducing the average amount of individual work space and increasing the amount of collaborative work space.

Direct structure is effective when the receiver is likely to agree with the main point of the message. That structure is also effective with receivers who are efficiency conscious—they want to know your main point immediately, whether or not they agree with it.

Indirect structure is patterned after inductive reasoning, which moves from specific examples or facts to generalized conclusions. The following paragraph illustrates indirect structure.

Last year's 15% increase in office staff has required us to examine the efficiency of our space usage. Since many employees already telecom-mute as many as three days a week, approximately 60% of our desks are vacant at one time. Instead of renting additional office space to accommodate staff growth, we will be redesigning the current office space. The goal is to reduce the average amount of individual work space and increase the amount of collaborative work space.

Consequently, in the office redesign, the number of individual work spaces will be reduced, and each space will be shared by two employees. The amount of common work space will be increased and will be appropriately configured for both individual and collaborative work as well as client meetings.

Indirect structure is effective for complex or controversial informa-tion. For such a message, the reader may need exposure to the detailed data before being able to understand and accept the conclusions and rec-ommendations of the report.

Business Reports Present Information Objectively

Since reports are used in the decision-making process, a user must be able to trust the information contained in a report. Objectivity refers to the selection of report content as well as to the presentation of that content. Deliberately excluding information that may be unpleasant to the writer or the receiver violates the objectivity criterion, which requires that all available relevant data be presented.

Report data may be drawn from a variety of sources. It is not uncommon for a report to contain observations of the person preparing it. For example, a manager may observe that employees are abusing the privilege of visiting social media sites while on the job; a report could follow in which the manager describes the observed practices and reminds the employees of a company policy related to conducting personal business on company time.

In another example, if an employee writes a trip report after attending a technical conference, much of the report content would be based on the employee's personal experiences during the trip; but the report likely would also include data about new products or techniques as well as facts about the costs incurred for travel, food, and lodging.

Similarly, as you report the status of a project, include objective statements about what has been accomplished and any difficulties encountered. If the project is behind schedule, include factual statements about what can or cannot be done to put it back on schedule, not your feelings that everyone should work hard and get the job done.

Although report writers may present personal observations or experiences in addition to impersonal facts, all information must be presented objectively—without distortion by feelings, opinions, or prejudices.

Business Reports Aid Decision Making

Some reports supply information necessary for decision making; others convey information about decisions that have been made and must be implemented. Since people at all levels of every organization must make or carry out decisions, reports are used in every kind of job. For example, a report may be as simple as a bank manager's oral reassignment of a teller from an inside workstation to a drive-up window after the manager observes that cars are lining up at the window. Or a report may be as complex as a retail store manager's written analysis of the store's operations, competition, and goals, concluding with a recommendation that the business be relocated.

The function of business reports in the decision-making process is shown in Figure 1.1, page 6.

The illustration suggests seven reports related to one business situation—entering an international market. The first report is an informal oral report by a sales associate of A&P, a (fictitious) U.S. manufacturer of gas grills, to the vice president for marketing. The sales associate recently returned from a vacation in Brazil, which is a significant regional producer and consumer of meats. While in Brazil, the sales associate noticed that many restaurants serve grilled-to-order meats—including lamb, beef, pork, fish, and fowl—and that many families enjoy outdoor grilling as well. However, the grilling is done primarily over charcoal. Although gas is readily available to homes and restaurants, the use of gas grills appears to be minimal. The sales associate thinks there is a potential opportunity to enter the Brazilian market with A&P's top-of-the-line gas grills.

The initial oral report by the sales associate could lead to a series of reports related to the feasibility of marketing gas grills in Latin America (see Figure 1.1). Those reports may be simple or complex, oral or written, formal or informal. Moreover, reporting occurs at every level of the organizational structure. Reports perform many functions in the organization, but the primary function is to improve the decision-making process and the quality of actions based on those decisions.

Classifications of Business Reports

Reports are not standardized messages. As the previous examples show, reports are used by many people, in many organizations, and for many purposes; consequently, reports take many forms. Report classifications can help you decide what type of report will best help you achieve your reporting objective. To understand the similarities and differences among reports, consider six ways in which reports may be classified: by function, frequency, subject matter, level of formality, reader–writer relationship, and communication medium.

Sender	Receiver	Report content	Report characteristics	Decision and action
A&P sales associate	A&P sales manager	Consumers in Brazil enjoy grilled meats; most use charcoal; potential market for our gas grills	Oral or e-mail; informal	Sales manager does preliminary research; relays information to vice president for marketing
Sales manager	Vice president for marketing	Burgeoning consumer market is attracting many U.S. companies to Brazil; few of our competitors are currently selling gas grills in Latin America	Written; semiformal; supplemented by oral summary	Vice president for marketing asks director of market research to conduct further research about feasibility of entering Latin American market
Vice president for marketing	Director of market research	Summary of previous reports; request to study feasibility of entering Latin American market	Written; semiformal	Director of market research assigns task to research staff; requests research proposal
Director of market research	Research staff	Summary of vice president's reports; requests for research proposal	Oral; informal; part of weekly staff meeting	Staff begins work on research proposal
Research staff	Director of market research	Proposed plan for feasibility study	Written; formal	Director approves plan; staff conducts study
Research staff	Director of market research	Findings, conclusions, recommendations of feasibility study	Formal; written; perhaps supplemented by oral presentation	Director asks staff to present report to management committee
Research staff and director of market research	Management committee	Background; summary of preliminary studies; findings, conclusions, recommendations of feasibility study	Oral and visual presentation; written summary of key findings and recommendations	Management authorization of budget for marketing division to begin efforts to establish distributorships in Brazil

Figure 1.1 Comparison of Various Report Types

Function

Reports typically serve one of two major functions: to inform or to analyze. An information report presents facts, observations, or experiences only. These facts or experiences may include requests for specific actions, such as the request for a feasibility study mentioned in Figure 1.1. The first five reports in that illustration are information reports.

An analytical report, sometimes called an examination report, identifies an issue or problem, presents relevant information, and interprets that information. The interpretation is often carried through to logical conclusion(s). The report may also offer recommendations for action. The last two reports in Figure 1.1 are analytical reports.

Frequency

Reports are often classified by frequency of transmission. Periodic reports are transmitted at stated times, such as daily, weekly, monthly, quarterly, or annually. A sales representative's weekly summary of calls is an example of a periodic report, as is a company's annual report to its stockholders. In contrast, a special report relates to a one-time or an infrequent event, such as the feasibility study mentioned in Figure 1.1. Another type of periodic report is a progress or status report, presented at appropriate intervals to inform decision makers about the status of an ongoing, usually large-scale project.

Subject Matter

Some organizations classify reports by broad subject areas that often correspond to functional divisions of the organization, such as accounting, production, finance, marketing, or engineering. Within the broad subject areas, narrower subject classifications may also exist: audit or tax reports within the accounting department or unit reports within the production division.

Level of Formality

Level of formality includes both tone and structure. In some contexts, formal tone and structure are expected; other contexts justify informality.

A formal report typically uses impersonal language and follows a prescribed format. Although formal reports may be written in memorandum or letter format, they are often presented in manuscript form. The format usually includes headings to guide you through the report content. If presented in manuscript format, the report generally includes a title page. As report length and complexity increase, other features, such as a table of contents and appendices, may be included. The final report of the feasibility study could well include a table of contents and appendices.

Informal reports project a more personal tone than do formal reports. First-person (I, we, us) and second-person (you) pronouns as well as near-conversational language may be used. Many informal reports are presented orally or in memorandum or letter format. In Figure 1.1, the sales associate's initial report to the sales manager is an informal report.

Reader–Writer Relationship

Reader–writer classification refers to the relationships that those parties have to one another. An internal report passes between a writer and reader in the same organization. Within an organization, other reader–writer relationships are suggested by terms such as management report, staff report, or committee report. All reports listed in Figure 1.1 are internal reports.

External reports move across organizational boundaries. A professional report by a consultant to the managers who employed the consultant is an example. Similarly, an audit report presented by an independent accounting firm to a client is an external report.

Communication Medium

When classified by the dominant communication tool or medium, reports are called written or oral, narrative or statistical, illustrated or unillustrated. Most report preparers use combinations of communication tools for multimedia reports. The last report listed in Figure 1.1 is an example of a multimedia report. This table does not cover the actual roll-out of A&P gas grills in the Brazilian market, which would involve connecting with customers and prospects via social media.

The classifications of reports demonstrate that reports are presented in many forms. Although report forms may vary, effective reports share common characteristics.

Characteristics of Effective Reports

Effective reports are understood by the receiver as the originator intended, and they influence the receiver to act as the report's creator desired. As the report maker, your objectives will be most likely achieved if they correspond with the needs and objectives of the recipient. An effective report involves empathy, accuracy, completeness, conciseness, and clarity. And effective reports present information ethically.

Empathy

Empathy is being sensitive to and vicariously experiencing the needs or feelings of another. A successful report creator attempts to understand the receiver's needs and fulfill those needs through report content, structure, and tone.

Most receivers of reports need to use their time economically. For written reports, for example, most readers want to skim, determining quickly what the report is about and its major points. You can demonstrate empathy with that need by supplying all necessary information in an easily comprehended structure. Coherent paragraph structure, logical organization, and use of headings, bullet points, or numbers help guide your readers and provide high skim value. Similarly, a courteous and respectful tone demonstrates empathy. Compare the following examples of nonempathetic versus empathetic writing. Although the nonempathetic example is a well-structured paragraph, its structure is hidden in the density of the text. In contrast, the empathetic example directs the reader's attention to each clearly stated recommendation.

Nonempathetic: After reviewing the plans to redesign our office space, I have several suggestions that may improve our employee's acceptance of the plans. First of all, schedule an e-conference at a time when most employees are able to participate to ensure that all employees get accurate information at the same time, thereby reducing rumors. Secondly, help employees appreciate the need for the office redesign by sharing the statistics about our current space usage and the costs associated with inefficient use of that space. Thirdly, assure employees that the office redesign will in no way impact our current telecommuting policy. This reassurance should relieve any concerns that employees may have about major changes in their current work styles. Finally, ease the discomfort that some employees may experience when confronting change by assuring them that their individual work styles, needs for communal space, and needs for private space with clients will be considered when work stations are assigned.

Empathetic: After reviewing the plans to redesign our office space, I have several suggestions that may improve our employees' acceptance of the plans:

1. Schedule an e-conference at a time when most employees are able to participate. Unpleasant rumors can best be avoided by giving all employees accurate information at the same time and allowing discussion of that information.
2. Share with the employees the statistics about our current space usage and the costs associated with inefficient use of that space. These statistics should help them appreciate the need for the office redesign.
3. Assure employees that the office redesign will not impact our current telecommuting policy. Employees must be confident that the office changes will have little effect on their current work styles.
4. Assure employees that their individual work styles, needs for communal space, and needs for private space with clients will be considered when work stations are assigned. This assurance should ease the discomfort that some employees may experience when confronting change.

Accuracy

Effective decisions can be made only if they are based on accurate information. Consequently, a primary criterion for effective reporting is accuracy.

The effective reporter attempts to gather accurate, objective data; verifies data when necessary; and presents the data accurately. Correct information is conveyed through accurate number use, word choice, spelling, grammar, and punctuation. Careful use of visuals also promotes correctness in understanding. Compare the following examples of incorrect and correct portions of reports.

Incorrect: The projected cost is $149.50; $60.00 for labor, $49.50 for materials, and $40.00 for indirect costs.

Correct: The projected cost is $149.50 per unit: $60.00 for labor, $49.50 for materials, and $40.00 for indirect costs.

OR

The projected per-unit cost is:

Labor	$60.00
Materials	$49.50
Indirect costs	$40.00
Total	$149.50

Completeness

Although completeness is an aspect of accuracy, it deserves special attention. Incomplete messages that omit essential data are likely to be inaccurate. Senders of incomplete messages tend to assume that the reader knows or will "fill in" certain details that the person, in reality, may not know or cannot supply. Consequently, receivers of incomplete messages often interpret them quite differently from the way the sender intended. Compare the following incomplete and complete presentations of information. Which versions are more effective?

Incomplete: The Lake Lure Artists welcome anyone who is interested in joining us. We meet on the second and fourth Thursdays of each month.

Complete: The Lake Lure Artists welcome anyone who is interested in joining us. We meet at 10 a.m. on the second and fourth Thursdays of each month in the Hickory Room of the Mugan Community Center.

OR

IMPORTANT NOTICE

What: Lake Lure Artists Meetings
When: Second and fourth Thursdays, 10 a.m.
Where: Hickory Room, Mugan Community Center

New members always welcome. Contact Lynn Blaine, 555-1234, for additional information.

Incomplete: Orders from Oxford Tool and Supply Company have declined during recent months. Please let me know soon what you plan to do to revive this account.

Complete: Orders from Oxford Tool and Supply Company for saw blades and router bits went down 10% each month during August, September, and October.

Please give me a detailed action plan for that account before November 15. Include in your plan the number of calls you have scheduled, whom you will contact, the questions you intend to ask, and the special offers, if any, you will make to revive that account.

Conciseness

Conciseness is a necessary complement to completeness. In an attempt to provide complete information, some report writers include more information than is necessary. An effective writer, however, uses the least number of words necessary to convey information accurately, completely, clearly, consistently, and empathetically. Concise writing is characterized by lack of trite expressions, redundancies, or unnecessary words. Compare the following examples.

Trite, commonplace expressions:
I look forward to serving you soon.
Let us supply all your hair needs.
Thank you in advance for your business.

Concise, relevant language:
I'll service your copier each Friday morning.
Hair Trimmers carries a complete selection of Head Turners shampoos and conditioners.
I would be pleased to provide your tax service during this new year.

Redundant: This report presentation provides the necessary information essential for reaching an informed decision regarding your plans and prospects for success in a profitable venture in that part of the city, that is, a new branch office.

Concise: This report provides information about the potential profitability of a branch office in the Shady Grove area.

Conciseness does not mean brevity above all; conciseness means avoiding unnecessary words. Compare the following examples of accurate, clear, empathetic, and concise writing with those that violate one or more of those criteria.

Concise but incomplete, nonempathetic: Call me tomorrow.

Concise, complete, empathetic: Please call me (555-5974) between 8 a.m. and 11:30 a.m. tomorrow.

Concise but incomplete: Amy's fee is less.

Concise and complete: Amy's fee is $500 less than Matt's.

Wordy, unclear, incorrect modification: Keeping in mind the objective of facilitating timely processing of rebate requests, it appears that a personnel increase in the neighborhood of 10% of our current staff will be essential.

Concise, clear, correct modification: To fulfill rebate requests promptly, we will need 20 additional employees.

A writer who supplies unnecessary or redundant information runs the risk of violating another criterion of effective reports: clarity.

Clarity

Since communication is an extremely complex process, the risk of misunderstanding is always present. This risk is compounded when communication occurs between people of different cultural background.

General Guides to Clarity

A general guide for clarity is to use simple rather than complex words, sentences, and paragraphs. Simple words are those that are familiar to both the sender and receiver. For example, most users of American English understand the words *dog* and *cat*, but fewer understand their synonyms *canine* and *feline*.

The relative simplicity of words is also related to the context in which they are used. Jargon, the technical or special language of a specific group, may simplify communication within that group; but when used with persons outside that group, jargon becomes a communication barrier. The following paragraph contains simple words; but to anyone other than a seasoned woodworker, it is probably meaningless:

> *Here's a way to dial in your miter gauge for tricky angles, such as for a seven-sided frame. Cut a piece of ¾" MDF wider than your miter gauge ... Then center a dado in one face to fit your miter-gauge bar, and add the base, support block, and hold-down.*[1]

Study the following examples of sentences using complex and simple words.

Complex: Subsequent to perusing the vendor's missive, Austin proclaimed his opposition regarding the egregious proposition.

Simple: After reading the seller's letter, Austin loudly rejected the extremely bad offer.

Another guide for clear writing is to use concrete, vivid words and descriptions rather than abstractions. Concrete words permit a narrow range of interpretation, while abstract words may be interpreted in many ways. For example, the abstract term electronic equipment may suggest objects as diverse as digital cameras, CD players, computers, and smartphones. But the concrete terms "computer and smartphone" are not likely to bring to mind images of a digital camera or a CD player. The following examples illustrate abstract and concrete language.

Abstract: Please return the questionnaire as soon as possible. Your responses are valuable to us and other consumers.

Concrete: Please complete and mail the questionnaire to 123 Blake Street, Citizen, OH 00000-0000, before April 30, 2017. Your responses will help us determine whether to add mobile banking to our array of customer services.

Sentence structure also contributes to or distracts from clarity. The simplest sentence follows the subject-verb-complement structure. That structure clearly identifies the actor, the action, and the receiver of the action, leaving little possibility of misinterpretation. However, excessive use of simple sentences can result in a choppy, nearly childlike writing style. An appropriate balance of simple sentences and longer, more complex sentences contributes to clear, interesting writing. Compare the following examples.

Complex: Because there was insufficient evidence of carrier responsibility, the carrier refused the damage claim that was filed by the customer only three days after the shipment arrived.

Too simple: The shipment arrived. Three days later the customer filed a damage claim. There was no evidence of carrier fault. The carrier refused the claim.

Appropriate balance: The customer filed a damage claim three days after the shipment arrived. The carrier refused that claim because there was no evidence of carrier fault.

Clear writing also requires correct use of pronouns. Indefinite pronoun reference—using a pronoun without a clear antecedent—destroys clarity because the reader or listener is not sure which noun is replaced by the pronoun. Compare the following examples.

Indefinite reference: After customers return the questionnaires to the company, they will analyze them.

Clear reference: After customers return the questionnaires to the company, the research staff will analyze the responses.

Indefinite reference: Ignoring customers' comments about unsatisfactory service will soon affect the bottom line. That is something we must correct immediately.

Clear reference: Ignoring customers' comments about unsatisfactory service will soon affect profits. We must respond to customers' comments promptly, and we must correct the service problems immediately.

An additional aspect of clarity is grammatical, structural, and logical consistency. Grammatical consistency (parallelism) exists when a writer uses the same grammatical structure for equivalent sentence or paragraph components. Compare the following examples of nonparallel and parallel grammatical structures.

Nonparallel: One day I would like to coach high school basketball and teach.

Parallel: One day I would like to coach high school basketball and be a teacher.

OR

One day I would like to be a high school coach and teacher.

OR

One day I would like to teach and coach basketball in a high school.

Nonparallel: Harter, Monk, and Ms. Adamson are analyzing the customer survey.

Parallel: Mr. Harter, Mr. Monk, and Ms. Adamson are analyzing the customer survey.

OR

Harter, Monk, and Adamson are analyzing the customer survey.

Structural consistency is achieved by maintaining the same structure for parallel units of a report. For example, the wording and placement of headings in a written report contribute to or distract from structural consistency. Compare the following examples of inconsistent and consistent headings in a report comparing purchased with free antivirus software.

Inconsistent:

1. Purchased antivirus software
   a. Firewall
   b. Parental controls
   c. Spam controls
   d. Browser toolbars to prevent phishing

2. Free
   a. No cost at start-up

    b. Less protection

    c. No technical support

Consistent:

  1. Purchased antivirus software

    a. Start-up costs

    b. Protection features

      Firewall?

      Parental controls?

      Spam controls?

      Antiphishing controls?

    c. Technical support

  2. Free antivirus software

    a. Start-up costs

    b. Protection features

      Firewall?

      Parental controls?

      Spam controls?

      Antiphishing controls?

    c. Technical support

Effective writers also strive to achieve logical consistency. Logic is a form of reasoning that imposes order on information. Logical reasoning contributes to truth, while fallacies (false or invalid arguments) distract from truth. Four common fallacies that report writers should avoid are *post hoc, ergo propter hoc* ("after this, therefore, because of this"); *non sequitur* ("it does not follow"); begging the question; and hasty generalization.

The *post hoc, ergo propter hoc* fallacy confuses passage of time with cause and effect. A writer guilty of this fallacy assumes that if one event occurred before another, the first event caused the second. Compare the following example of a *post hoc, ergo propter hoc* fallacy with the logical statement that follows it. Note that the complete, correct logical statement is longer than the fallacy. Logical consistency should not be sacrificed for conciseness.

Post hoc, ergo propter hoc: District *A* sales have increased 1% each month since Sanchez became district manager. He has turned that territory around.

Logical statement: Although economic conditions have not changed in District A, its sales have increased 1% each month since Sanchez became district manager. He has personally helped each sales representative develop a sales plan. That management technique appears to have improved the district's performance.

A *non sequitur* states a conclusion based on faulty or insufficient evidence. The following sentences contrast a *non sequitur* with a logical statement.

Non sequitur: We received 200 calls in response to Sunday's newspaper advertisement. Our sales are sure to pick up this month.

Logical statement: We received 200 calls in response to Sunday's newspaper advertisement. If only 10% of those respondents order by February 28, February's sales will be 2% above January's.

Begging the question is a fallacy in which an assumption or conclusion is restated instead of being supported by logical reasons or evidence. "I should be more assertive because I need to assert myself" merely repeats the need to be assertive but does not supply a reason. "I need to be more assertive because people often take advantage of me" supplies a reason for the conclusion. The following example further contrasts begging the question with a logical statement.

Begging the question: I rejected this proposal because I cannot accept it in its present form.
Logical statement: I rejected this proposal because the cost data were incomplete.

In a hasty generalization, a person reasons that because something is true in some instances, it is true in the case under discussion. Compare the following examples.

Hasty generalization: Sandy has more education than any other applicant. Sandy is the best person for this position.

Logical statement: Sandy scored higher than any other applicant on all selection criteria. Sandy is the best applicant for this position.

Grammatical consistency, structural consistency, and logical consistency improve report clarity. Moreover, presenting data and conclusions logically makes a report and its creator believable, whereas fallacies tend to cast doubt on the report content and its originator.

As you compose reports, evaluate your writing by the criteria of empathy, accuracy, completeness, conciseness, and clarity. Those criteria are exemplified in the e-mail shown in Figure 1.2, page 21.

Notice that the e-mail fits the characteristics of a report: It is an organized, objective presentation of a fact, and it is written to influence action. The organizational structure is evidenced by headings as well as numbered and bulleted items. The organization and format help the reader easily focus on the main points (skim value), thereby demonstrating empathy for the reader. The tone of the message, courteous yet firm, also demonstrates empathy. Beginning with the description of the problem adds to the accuracy and completeness of the data, helping the reader understand the importance of the requested action. Notice that the language is clear and concrete, avoiding such trite expressions as "It has come to our attention that …." The requested action is also written in clear, concise language, providing a concrete procedure to be followed. The comment about expected results again demonstrates empathy, showing that the requested action will benefit the reader of the e-mail, not just the sender.

Guides to Clarity Across Cultures

When your identified audience includes people for whom English is not the native language, even more care is necessary to make your writing clear

Customer service etiquette, training update
To: Managers Group@quik-host.com
Cc: Gerald Montero@quik-host.com
Subject: Customer Service Etiquette, Training Update

Problem Encountered
 	
Quik-Host hired Secret Shoppers to evaluate customer service in Quik-Host stores. Recent reports from Secret Shoppers show that some Quik-Host cashiers keep a customer waiting at the counter while the cashier processes a phone call coming into the store.
 	
Required Action
 	
Please remind all cashiers that a customer standing at a counter *always* takes precedence over the store's incoming calls. Review with your employees this procedure to be followed when a call comes in while a customer is at the cashier's counter. (Calls on an employee's mobile phone should not be answered until his or her break.)
 	
1. Complete the transaction with the customer at the counter before answering the phone.
2. If no other employee has answered the phone after four rings:
  • Say to the customer, "Please excuse me while I take this call."
  • Answer the phone, saying, "Thank you for calling Quik-Host. Please hold briefly."
  • Immediately put the caller on hold; page another employee to take the call.
  • Return to your customer; apologize for the interruption.
  • Complete the transaction with the customer.
  • If the call is still on hold, take the call and apologize for the wait.
 	
Expected Results
 	
This procedure shows respect for visitors at your store while maintaining goodwill with each caller, who may be a potential customer or supplier. We all benefit when our customers are treated well.
 	
Harold Sweetman
VP-Corporate Marketing

Figure 1.2 Report Characteristics Demonstrated

to them. First, learn as much as you can about the cultural expectations of the people you are writing to or for. Will they, like most U.S. business people, appreciate direct, concise writing as a courteous time-saver; or will they see direct and concise as rude—your way of getting done as fast as you can? Consider deeper issues, too. Will the audience prefer direct or indirect structure, particularly when you convey what readers may view as negative or unfavorable?[2]

About 1.5 billion people of Earth's 7.3 billion people speak English well enough to use the language for business, but less than a third of these (400 million) speak and read English as their first, or native, language.[3] In his book, *The Elements of International English*, Edmond Weiss refers to native readers and speakers of English as E1s. (English is their first language.) Those persons who read and speak English as a second (or later) language Weiss calls E2s, noting that the proportion of E2s to world population is increasing while the proportion of E1s is decreasing. Weiss gives advice to anyone who writes for the large, growing number of E2s.[4]

Weiss's advice for writing to an intercultural audience involves two main principles:

1. Reduce the burden on E2 readers every way you can, without dumbing down; that is, without lowering the intellectual content.
2. Write for translation; that is, for a reader who might consult a bilingual dictionary.[5]

The clarity rules included in the previous pages generally apply when writing for E2s. But you can do more.

Sentence-Level Adaptations. The burden on E2 readers is reduced when the writer uses the simplest form of verbs. Other adaptations include avoiding phrasal verbs, eliminating dangling phrases, and omitting elliptical sentences.

- Use a verb's simplest form. As noted previously, active verbs aid clarity better than passive verbs do. Clarity requires omitting verbs that express a desire, improbability, supposition, or wish—what grammarians call subjunctive mood.[6] And avoid verbs that express commands (imperative mood), which may come across as bossy or rude to an E2 reader. Examples follow.

Subjunctive mood: If you **were to train** media employees to design newsletters, you will likely see more employees reading them. It is necessary that newsletters **be** published on Tuesday or Wednesday morning—never on Monday or Friday.

Imperative mood: **Find** a document design expert to do the training. **Set up** a training schedule.

- Avoid phrasal verbs. In using short, simple words, avoid phrasal (multiple-word) verbs, such as make up, pay out, speed up, think about, and work out. Instead, use a single word synonym: fabricate, disburse, accelerate, contemplate, and calculate or determine.[7]
- Eliminate dangling phrases. When using an infinitive phrase (to recommend) or a phrase based on a participle (recommending) at the beginning or end of a sentence, ensure the phrase does not dangle. That is, connect the infinitive or participle phrase in meaning to the word or phrase immediately before or after it.[8] Examples follow:

Incorrect: To increase citizens' support for the proposed relocation of the cruise terminal, an extensive communication campaign must be launched by the State Port Authority.

Correct: To increase citizens' support for the proposed relocation of the cruise terminal, the State Port Authority must launch an extensive communication campaign.

Note: The preceding sentence could have been written as follows: … the proposed cruise terminal relocation…. But when writing for E2s, avoid long strings of words vital to meaning.

Incorrect: Working late every night last week, the report was finished ahead of schedule.

Correct: Working late every night last week, the team finished the report ahead of schedule.

- Omit elliptical sentences. The general guide to clarity says to use short, simple sentences. But the needs of E2 readers often dictate using longer sentences with implied or elliptical words left in, as shown in the following examples.[9]

Chase is a reticent coworker, but a dynamic presenter.

Chase is a reticent coworker, but he is a dynamic presenter.

Elaine senses she was wrong about the research results.

Elaine senses that she was wrong about the research results.

I sent nine of my progress reports on time; three, late.

I sent nine of my progress reports on time; three reports were sent late.

One team member likes revising reports better than drafting them.

One team member likes revising reports better than she likes drafting them.

When asked about status of the project, the team leader evaded the question.

When she was asked about status of the project, the team leader evaded the question.

Word-Level Adaptations. English translation is easier when the writer uses words that have few meanings. And English text becomes more translatable when confusing words are double- and triple-checked for accuracy. The burden for E2 readers is greatly reduced when English text is culture-free; that is, it contains no literary references to British or American culture; no business jargon, including military and sports allusions, and no classic idioms.

- Use words with the fewest meanings, even if doing so requires a longer word.[10] For example, at the time this book was written, the words "run" and "set" each had over 30 definitions in the *Merriam-Webster Unabridged Dictionary*. The bilingual dictionaries that E2 readers often use typically contain only the first one or two definitions of such words. So to avoid confusion, choose a synonym with fewer meanings, and do not use contractions, such as don't or we've. Also, omit short versions of long words, such as ad for advertisement, info for information, and tech for technology.[11]

- Take extra care to use homophones (same-sounding words with different meanings) correctly. Examples include hear and here and their and there. Alan Cooper's list of homophones (often called homonyms) (www.cooper.com/alan/homonym. html) includes hundreds of sound-alikes in American English.
- Some similar-sounding words (adapt, adept, adopt; proceed, precede) require careful attention. And beware of common typos, such as form and from. As you may know, spelling-checker software simply compares your string of characters to a list of acceptable strings. Thus, the spelling-checker will not catch errors resulting from one real word being substituted for another.
- Make your text culture-free. Avoid references to literary works and artifacts embedded in your culture.[12] A few examples follow:

Literary references from British and American culture
- Big brother (from Orwell's *1984*)
- Blood on my hands (from Shakespeare's *Macbeth*)
- Catch-22 (from Heller's book with this title)
- Discretion is the better part of valor (from Shakespeare's *Henry IV*)
- Scrooge (from Dickens' *A Christmas Carol*)

Sayings and scriptural references
- A good paymaster never wants workmen.
- (Don't) cast pearls before swine.
- If it ain't broke, don't fix it.
- Love of money is the root of all evil.
- Don't hide your light under a bushel.
- The best things in life are free.

Pop culture references
- Breaking bad
- It takes a village
- New world order
- Post a selfie
- It takes two to tango

- Omit common U.S. business jargon that may not translate for business people from a different background. Likewise, leave out the military and sports allusions common in U.S. business language.

    Business jargon:
    - Blue sky thinking
    - Going forward
    - Leverage
    - Millennial generation
    - Synergy
    - Utilize
    - Value added

    Military and sports allusions:
    - Boots on the ground
    - Deploy all available troops
    - See some collateral damage
    - Drop back and punt
    - Dropped the ball
    - Threw a curveball

- Omit classic idioms that native English speakers understand and use automatically, without thinking. According to the *Merriam-Webster Dictionary*, an idiom is an expression that cannot be understood from the meanings of its separate words but that has a separate meaning of its own. Nonnative English speakers often cannot relate to idioms,[13] and bilingual dictionaries do not help readers who consult them to translate English idioms.

Idiom included: Team members agreed they should go back to the drawing board before collecting data.

Idiom omitted: Team members agreed they should plan the study again before collecting data.

Idiom included: The managers who interviewed saw him as a diamond in the rough.

Idiom omitted: The managers who interviewed him saw him as lacking polish but having great potential.

In *Word Watcher's Handbook* (2001), author Phyllis Martin listed more than 900 of these trite expressions.[14] An updated list would likely contain many of the same phrases, along with some new ones.

- Omit slang and trendy words in your culture that could prove illegible to readers unfamiliar with the words. Use standard English rather than any slang expressions that may be in vogue.[15] Such terms tends to be short-lived anyway. Text to be read by a global audience should omit trendy words and acronyms used in social media, even though business people in various cultures participate in Facebook, Twitter, Instagram, Snapchat, and others.

Other Adaptations. Punctuation—especially commas and hyphens—can be employed to make text more translatable. Also use care in expressing dates and money. Use commas in places where commas are now considered optional in American English: after an introductory phrase as well as after an introductory clause, and before and, or, or nor in a series.[16] For example:

In addition information related to water-front development was studied.
In addition, information related to water-front development was studied.
Note: When writing for E2s, a hyphen in compound nouns, such as waterfront, aids clarity.
This area includes the downtown retail, hospitality and professional facilities.
This area includes the downtown retail, hospitality, and professional facilities.

- Use semicolons between items in a series that already contain commas: Surat, India; Detroit, Michigan USA; Milan, Italy; and Melbourne, Australia.
- Use a hyphen between a prefix, such as anti, mis, non, over, pre, semi, and trans and the word following it, although the combination may appear as one word in your English: anti-freeze, mis-fire, non-sense, over-look, pre-treat, semi-circle, and trans-continental.[17]
- Take extra care in expressing money and dates. For example, in the U.S., 07/10/17 means July 10, 2017. In other places, it may mean October 7.

In the United States, numbers over 999 are punctuated with commas to separate hundreds from thousands, thousands from millions, millions from billions, and so forth: 4,567; 4,567,890 and so on. And in money amounts a decimal point separates dollars from cents: $4,567.89; $456,789.01; $4,567,890.41 and so forth.[18] In European and Latin American countries, the convention is reversed: Decimal points separate hundreds from thousands and so on, while commas separate dollars from cents: 4.000; 4.765.321; €10.987,65; €432.109,87; and €65,43. Notes: Except in tables, type even money amounts without the decimal point and two zeros. In running text, a clearer way to express numbers and money amounts over 999,999 is this convention that involves a combination of numerals and words: 4.568 million, $6 billion, and $1.2 trillion.

The $ symbol is known as the dollar sign and the peso sign. Besides the United Sates, the following countries use this sign before money amounts: Australia, Canada, Fiji, Hong Kong, Liberia, Namibia, Singapore, Suriname, Tuvalu, and many—but not all—Latin American countries. To aid clarity, specify which country's dollar you mean by inserting the ISO currency code in parentheses after the amount, as in USD for US dollars, HKD for Hong Kong dollars, and AUD for Australian dollars. Notes: XE Trade publishes symbols for most world currencies (www.xe.com/symbols.php) and a list of ISO codes for all of the world's currencies (www.xe.com/iso4217.php).

The symbols for Europe's euros (€), Britain's pound (£), and Japan's yen (¥) are available in the symbol sets of most word processing software.

Another easy way to insert the most common currency symbols into your text is Szynalski's TypeIt website (currencies.typeit.org/).

Removing unnecessary burdens and increasing translatability of English text is an act of empathy by the writer for the benefit of a global reading audience. When you write for international readers, step back from your deep-rooted habits and focus on strategies that show your respect for them.

A final element of reporting must be considered: the ethical dimension.

Ethicality

Since the objective of any report is to bring about good decisions, the writer has an ethical responsibility. Consider the complexities of the situation described in Case 1.1:

Case 1.1 Ethical complexity of reports

Most people agree that persons or organizations that are in a position to influence the lives of others ought to behave ethically—they should "do the right thing." But "oughts" or "shoulds" are themselves ethical judgments, indicating the complexity of the ethical arena. Assume that you have observed safety violations in the manufacturing plant in which you work. You decide to prepare a report in which you will identify each violation and recommend corrections.

- Is your purpose to improve working conditions or to expose lax management? Will you present both sides of the issue?
- Should your audience be upper management, or should it include employees and the press?
- What tone should you use; that is, what attitude should you show toward receivers of the report?
- Should the report be released if your analysis of context reveals that an environmental interest group in the

community is attempting to have the plant closed—even though many community members would lose their jobs?
- Should the report disclose all violations you have observed or only selected ones? Which medium—oral or written—would yield greater "good"?

Some dilemmas are more complex than others. For simpler quandaries related to report creation, following the guidelines in Figure 1.3 will serve you well.

When submitting a research proposal—

- Submit solicited proposals only if you are able to satisfy the requester's needs.

- Include qualifications of the person(s) who will conduct the study—a demonstration of competence to fulfill the proposal.

- Include specific techniques for protecting the confidentiality of participants in the project.

- In unsolicited proposals, address ONLY genuine, verifiable problems that you can analyze competently.

When collecting business data—

- Enter a database or electronic file to obtain information only if the database or file is yours or you have authorization in writing to access it. Otherwise, it is burglary or theft.

- Avoid any secretive data collection methods, such as monitors in store fitting rooms to observe shoppers' behavior. And observe the Federal Trade Commission's Telemarketing Sales Rule—all to prevent violating a person's fundamental right to privacy, guaranteed in the Fourth Amendment.

- In general, when conducting primary research, use the most powerful data sampling techniques available to you within your time and monetary budgets to help ensure accurate conclusions m your study.

- Consider the importance of your research problem before choosing a sampling procedure. An inexpensive, easy-to-use convenience sample of individuals entering a store may be adequate to test consumers' initial reactions, but a more difficult, costly stratified random sample would be better for identifying the target market prior to launching a marketing campaign.

When analyzing business research data—

- Analyze all available, relevant data, even data that will not support your viewpoint or provide an outcome that you know the study's authorizer prefers.

- Before analyzing primary data statistically, set a practical level of statistical significance. Your findings may be significant at the .10 (10%) level but not at the .05 (5%) or .01 (1%) level. Ethics would be questionable if you were to claim statistical significance when there is a 10% probability that observed relationships or differences are merely chance observations.

When creating report visuals—

- Keep in mind that visuals typically have more impact than the text accompanying them because (1) visuals have emotional impact that words lack; (2) skimmers see visuals even when they do not read the text; and (3) people remember visuals longer.

- Avoid distortion by attending carefully to scale dimensions and sizes of symbols (bars, circles, boxes, etc.) used in your visuals.

- Make every visual complete, including titles and labels.

- On bar and line charts, make the distance equal between all units of measurement on each axis (some exceptions apply).

When preparing a research-based report—

- If you were unable to analyze all possible elements of a research problem or your available data sources are less than ideal, include in your report an honest statement of delimitations (boundaries you have set for the study) and limitations (conditions you cannot control that restrict your conclusions or influence research results). Explain each delimitation and limitation.

- Accurately credit information and ideas obtained from both primary sources, including company records or employee interviews, and secondary sources, such as journal articles and websites.

- When obtaining information from the web, credit copyrighted material as meticulously as information obtained from a book or journal article.

- On a team, as each member credits data sources used in his or her section, all members must be alert to the possibility that a writer, knowingly or unknowingly, has not credited sources adequately.

- If you promised primary data sources that they would not be identified in your report, fulfill that promise by presenting information in such a way that the data cannot be traced to specific participants.

- Test the logic of conclusions drawn from research findings and examine the likely impact of your recommendations.

When delivering an oral report—

- Do NOT exaggerate a point, omit something crucial, or provide deceptive emphasis in order to make the point more forceful. The resulting deception destroys a speaker's credibility.

Figure 1.3 Guides to Ethical Reporting

Both individuals and organizations develop ethical systems or frameworks to achieve some degree of consistency and consensus about what is good and right when facing complex dilemmas. Bruce Weinstein, also known as The Ethics Guy, provides these maxims for ethical behavior:[19]

- Do no harm
- Make things better
- Respect others
- Be fair
- Be compassionate

More often than not, ethical questions concern right versus right rather than right versus wrong. Right-versus-right questions vary in complexity and cannot be resolved with easy solutions such as "do the right thing." Weinstein suggests that when conflicts arise between right and right, the closer someone is to you, the stronger is your duty to do no harm, make things better, and act with respect, fairness, and compassion.

Another ethicist, Joseph Badaracco, devised a four-question model for dealing with right-versus-right problems:[20]

1. What are the consequences of different ways of dealing with the problem for everybody who will be affected by the decision? In other words, which course of action will do the most good and the least harm?
2. What individuals and groups involved in the situation have rights that you must respect? Which of your alternatives best serves others' rights, including those of your organization's shareholders?
3. What messages do you want to send about your values as a leader and the values of your organization? Ask yourself, what plan can I live with that is consistent with basic values and commitments?
4. What's going to make a difference in the real world? In a word, which of your alternatives will work?

As Badaracco acknowledged, managers may lack the time for the in-depth analysis these four questions entail. Therefore, he condensed the questions into a short version, consisting of three tests: the newspaper test, the golden rule test, and the best-friend test.[21]

1. *Newspaper test*: Ask yourself how you would deal with the problem in front of you if it's going to appear on your local paper's front page

tomorrow morning. This test focuses on the consequences of your action and its practicality.

2. *Golden rule test*: Take the Native American advice to walk a mile in other people's shoes. What would your action be if you were in the other person's place? Thus, you can focus on others' rights that you may otherwise overlook in your haste to make a decision.

3. *Best-friend test*: Imagine someone who knows you well and whose respect matters to you looking back a few years from now on the pending decision and how you made it. How do you feel about your choice? This test puts a spotlight on character—yours and that of the organization you are serving or shaping.

Understanding frameworks for moral judgments, such as those proposed by Weinstein and Badaracco, will help you understand how and why your decisions sometimes differ from those of other well-meaning, moral, rational people. Using ethical models to direct judgments made during the communication process can improve the ethical quality of your writing and help you produce more effective reports.

As you finalize a comprehensive report, use the following criteria as a checklist of ethical considerations about the content you have presented.

Did you:
- Verify the need for the research?
- Report all relevant data?
- Avoid manipulative language?
- Honor the privacy, accuracy, and ownership guides related to data sources?
- Honor your commitments to survey participants to maintain confidentiality?
- Avoid distortion of data in your visual aids?

A final question about your work might well be this: Does this report represent my best effort to convey information that will promote the good of others as I remain true to my own values and ideals?

Summary

Reports can be defined as organized, objective presentations of observations, experiences, or facts. Their basic function is to provide information for effective decisions and actions at all levels of an organization. Effective reports contribute to the advancement of the reporter's career as well as to the success of the organization.

As you undertake your reporting activities, build in empathy, accuracy, completeness, conciseness, clarity, and ethicality as you plan, draft, and revise each report. Use the following checklist to evaluate all your reports.

- ☐ Does your report accommodate the audience's needs and feelings, including a courteous, respectful tone, and—in written reports—time-saving features, such as logical organization, use of headings and bulleted and numbered lists, and coherent paragraphs?
- ☐ Does your report include correct grammar, number usage, punctuation, spelling, word choice, and visuals?
- ☐ Does your report include all information needed by the audience to bring about the report's purpose?
- ☐ Does your report omit trite expressions, redundancies, and unnecessary words?
- ☐ Does your report use simple, concrete, vivid words and descriptions; a balance of simple and complex sentences; an antecedent for each pronoun; parallel grammatical structure; structural consistency in report headings; and logical consistency throughout?
- ☐ If writing for an international audience, did you use the simplest form of verbs, words with the fewest meanings, well-placed commas and hyphens, and meticulous notation for dates and money amounts?
- ☐ Does that report also omit multiple-word verbs, dangling phrases, and elliptical sentences?

☐ And does your report for the international audience omit errors in the use of homophones and other confusing words?

☐ Also, is your report culture-free, omitting literary references, business jargon, military and sports allusions, and classic idioms?

☐ Does your report conform to a standard of what is right and good, leading to respectable decisions and actions?

CHAPTER 2

Planning and Organizing Business Reports

A well-planned report contributes to effective communication, whereas a hastily written report frequently leads to misunderstanding. Some reports require only brief informal plans. Consider, for example, a one-page memo to employees reporting that management has approved an extra holiday for all employees. A manager could easily write this report after reviewing notes made in a managers' meeting; but the good writer would take time to consider the audience, desired effect of the report, exact information to be included, and order of presentation.

In contrast, consider a report from a market researcher to a management committee about a recently completed market survey. Before writing the report, the researcher would develop a formal plan that likely would be presented to a supervisor for evaluation, suggestions, and approval. That plan would include factors such as the intended audience for the report, the purpose of the study, a full description of how the research was conducted, and the results. As a general guide, the formality and length of the report plan are directly related to the complexity of the information to be reported.

Planning a Written Report

Strong report writers follow a six-step plan before beginning to write, as shown in Figure 2.1.

Although report writers sometimes follow these steps in the order listed, the dotted lines in the illustration indicate that the process is recursive, not linear. The elements are interdependent. For example, identification of the context may help to identify the audience, identification of the purpose may help to define the content, and identification of the content and audience should contribute to selection of the appropriate medium.

Identify purpose	Why?
↓	↓
Identify audience	Who?
↓	↓
Identify context	Where
↓	↓
Identify content	What
↓	↓
Select medium	How?
↓	↓
Choose report structure	What relationships?

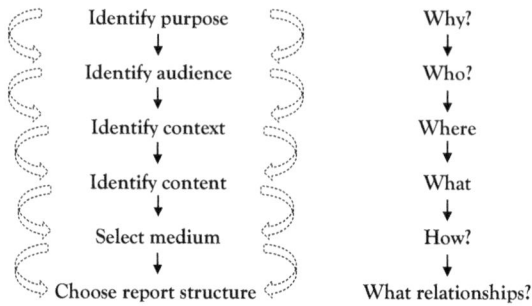

Figure 2.1 Six-Step Writing Plan

Identify Purpose

In some instances, the motivation for the report is that your job description requires you to submit such a report. For example, a sales representative may be required to present a weekly report of calls made, contracts acquired, and plans for the following week. Whether prompted by your job description or by special circumstances, the report will be most successful if you define your purpose in terms of what you want your reader to do or think after reading it. If you do not define the desired outcome, the report may become nothing more than a presentation of data; you will place the burden of interpretation on the reader. The reader may well conclude that action is necessary, but the action may not be what you expected.

Reports can be classified according to their general purposes: production, innovation, or goodwill.[1] Production messages relate to getting the job done. Assigning an employee a new area of responsibility or reporting a deviation from production standards are examples of production messages. Innovation messages relate to initiating change in an organization. A proposal to split an operating division into two units or a memo explaining a company's newly adopted telecommuting policy are examples of innovation messages. Goodwill messages relate to maintaining the loyalty and morale of the people within or outside the organization. Reports about employee accomplishments or plans for the company picnic are examples of goodwill reports. Most short, simple reports are production messages dealing with a single, clearly definable topic and an objective that relates directly to accomplishing the organization's tasks.

A sales representative's weekly production report, for example, tells a sales manager about the progress the representative is making toward achieving sales goals; and a policy statement about drug use tells employees what can, must, and will be done to maintain a productive working environment.

By its very nature, innovation often requires review of a problem or presentation of a rationale that requires or justifies an organizational change. For that reason, a well-structured message that will persuade a reader to accept change may require greater length and formality than is typically associated with many short reports. However, context and audience could also justify a relatively short report for an innovation message. For example, a complete analysis of the benefits and disadvantages of telecommuting might be presented in a lengthy, formal report to management, while management's report to employees about the new telecommuting policy could be written in a page or two.

Managers also write short reports for goodwill purposes. A report about employees' volunteer activities with local hospitals or a report identifying and congratulating top sales associates for the month would be written primarily to reinforce the employees' sense of self-worth and value to the organization—to maintain employee morale.

As you plan your report, it is useful to identify the general purpose as production, innovation, or goodwill. This identification will help you determine the specific purpose (for example, to report last week's sales, to gain approval for a new policy, or to congratulate employees for participation in the United Way campaign), as well as the appropriate content, structure, writing style, and tone for the message.

Consider the following Case 2.1 that illustrates the importance of message planning.

Case 2.1 Crafting a negative employee write-up

Your company, which develops computer software for the insurance industry, has a sick-leave policy. This policy specifically requires employees to inform their supervisors before 8:30 a.m. if they are ill and unable to report to work. The policy allows 1.5 days of leave per month, which may accumulate up to 36 days of sick leave. If employees are suspected of misusing the benefit, they may be required to submit medical proof of illness.

One of your employees, Janice Widener, has recently taken a part-time, moonlighting job with a start-up software firm that has been somewhat secretive about the type of software it is working on. The job requires her to work from 6 p.m. until 10 p.m. on Tuesdays and Thursdays. Since taking that job, Widener has frequently called in sick on Wednesday or Friday. She has averaged one sick day per week, sometimes two mornings. You have also observed that she often seems sluggish on days following her evening work hours. As her supervisor, you have spoken with her about her absences and her lackluster performance, but the pattern persists. When you questioned her about her frequent sick days, she said there should be no problem because she had accumulated 15 days of leave.

You now plan to report the situation to the director of human resources. Answer the following questions before preparing your report:

1. What do you want the HR director to do: Counsel Widener? Make an entry in Widener's personnel records? Advise you about ways to motivate Widener to stop that behavior?
2. How will your decision about the report's purpose influence other reporting steps, such as identification of content and structure and selection of an appropriate medium?

Identify Audience

Before preparing your report, you must identify your audience, both primary and secondary. In Case 2.1, the primary receiver is the human resources director to whom you will send the report. Secondary readers may be current and future human resources staff or higher-level managers—and perhaps Widener herself.

Audience identification requires more than merely identifying who will receive the report. After identifying the primary receiver, try to empathize with that person and identify her or his information and ego needs. If your purpose complements those needs, your writing task is relatively easy. But if your purpose contradicts the receiver's needs, your task becomes more difficult. In such a situation, before you state the main point of your report, you will have to give enough information to overcome possible objections in the receiver's mind.

Consider again Case 2.1. One need of the human resources director is to be well informed about all personnel issues. You may also know that the director is altruistic (that is, desires to help others); and as a busy manager, the director likely prefers clear, concise, complete messages that permit immediate action without further clarification. As a good report writer, you will satisfy all those needs by indicating clearly what you want the director to do, including all necessary information to support that request and excluding unnecessary details. Knowing that the director is altruistic, you might word the request to show that the desired action will help Widener, you, or other employees.

Although your first concern is to address the primary reader, recognize also that others may read the report. Even if you and the human resources director are well acquainted, considering the possible secondary readers should prevent you from using an excessively personal or casual tone in the report. The possibility that Widener herself may have access to the report or that it may become evidence in a disciplinary action should also prompt you to avoid emotional or abstract terms. The report must be objective and unambiguous.

Identify Context

The report context includes the physical and psychological environment of the communication exchange. Many reports are transmitted routinely with little thought about the context in which the message will be received. Many businesspeople, for example, feel burdened by the plethora of daily e-mails, many of which demonstrate little concern for the physical or emotional context in which the message is received. Effective communicators send their reports, whether written or electronic, to arrive at a time and place that will encourage the reader to give full attention to the message.

If, for example, you know that the human resources director always has a management meeting on Monday morning, you might be wise to ensure that the director receives the report about Widener on Wednesday or Thursday. That timing would permit the director to dispose of tasks related to the previous Monday's management meeting and give full attention to the report. Appropriate timing would allow the director to consider appropriate action, including what—if anything—about the case should be discussed at the next management meeting. Or assume that you decide to give Widener a final oral warning before reporting her absences and erratic performance. The appropriate place and time for that warning would be privately in your office or at Widener's work station immediately after you observe her breakdown in performance—not at her annual review several months later.

Identify Content

Identifying purpose, audience, and context will help you determine appropriate content for your report. You must include all information the receiver requires to fulfill your purpose, as well as details that motivate the receiver to act. Just as important, however, is the caution to exclude unnecessary details that may obstruct understanding. Include all the receiver must know, not necessarily all you know or find interesting. Exclude any information that is not relevant to the purpose of the report.

If, for example, your purpose is to stimulate the human resources director to discipline Widener, you must provide all information justifying such action: a record of Widener's infractions, what you have done to correct the situation, Widener's responses to your actions, and the effects of her behavior. You should not, however, include comments about your personal dislike of Widener or rumors about her plans to leave your company and work full-time for her current part-time employer.

Another critical part of your report-writing plan is to choose a medium to transmit the report.

Select Medium

Media differ in their ability to transmit information. About 30 years ago, Lengel and Daft developed the medium richness theory, which classifies a medium as rich or lean on the basis of its ability to meet three criteria: transmit multiple cues, facilitate rapid feedback, and provide a personal focus (see Figure 2.2). This theory has stood the test of time and has been supported by extensive research.[3]

Media Richness			
Richest >>>>>>>>>>>>>>>>>>>>>>>>>>>>>>>>>>>>>> Least Rich			
Physical Presence Face-to-face discussion, oral presentation with question–answer session	Interactive Media Phone, e-mail, instant messaging, audio- and video-conferencing	Personal Static Media Memo, letter, report in personal style	Impersonal Static Media Flyers, bulletins, posters, worksheet printout, general-ized report

Figure 2.2 Media Richness Continuum[2]

As shown, the richest medium is face-to-face communication because it meets all three criteria. Impersonal media, such as flyers or bulletin-board announcements, are lean. They can accommodate few cues, allow for delayed feedback only, and have no personal focus. Memos, letters, and reports tailored for a specific receiver are richer than bulletins because they have a more personal focus even though they do not permit imme-diate feedback.

E-mail is somewhat richer than printed letters or memoranda; while permitting a personal focus, it also enables more rapid feedback than does a printed letter or memorandum. On his E-mail Overload blog, Michael Einstein wrote that e-mail was believed to be a lean medium, accord-ing to original media richness theory: "[E-mail] is text-based, asynchro-nous in nature, and incapable of transmitting non-textual cues, such as facial expressions, body language, and tone." But the blogger stated that later studies challenged this notion: E-mail can create a rich interaction between senders and recipients.[4]

Interactive media, such as phones, online conferences, or instant mes-saging, are richer than are memos, letters, or e-mail because the interactive options permit both a personal focus and immediate feedback. Although some interactive media (for example, videoconferencing) can accommo-date both visual and vocal cues, others (for example, phones) cannot. No interactive medium is as rich as face-to-face communication, which can accommodate the full range of vocal and visual cues.

Research has shown that using lean media for communicating about routine management problems and richer media for nonroutine problems contributes to communication success. In contrast, using a lean medium for a nonroutine problem contributes to communication breakdown. Lean media provide too few cues for the message receiver, resulting in information shortage. Similarly, using a rich medium for a routine problem tends to cause communication breakdown because the message provides excess cues, resulting in information overload or noise (see Figure 2.3).

Consider again Case 2.1 and Janice Widener's absences and lackluster performance on days following her night job. The first time you approach Widener to report that this behavior must change, you would probably use face-to-face communication for this nonroutine message. Posting a notice on the bulletin board reminding employees of the sick-leave policy would likely have little effect on Widener because the medium is too impersonal. On the contrary, an e-mail (or memo if the director prefers that medium) would be an appropriate means to report Widener's behavior to human resources. Neither you nor the director needs immediate feedback, but the e-mail can be personalized and—if printed—can become part of Widener's personnel file. A telephone call or a face-to-face conversation could result in miscommunication. The richness of those media could overemphasize the significance of a problem that is routine

Media richness	Management problem	
	Routine	Nonroutine
Rich ↓ Lean	Communication failure Rich medium used for routine situation • Too much data • Excess cues cause confusion, distort meaning	Communication success Rich medium used for nonroutine situation • Allows sufficient data • Number, kinds of cues signal significance of message
	Communication success Lean medium used for routine situation • Sufficient data • No excess cues to distract receiver	Communication failure Lean medium used for nonroutine situation • Insufficient data • Number, kinds of cues downplay significance of message

Figure 2.3 Media Selection by Richness[5]

to most human resources directors, who handle such situations as part of their normal duties. Moreover, although a phone call or a face-to-face conversation permits immediate feedback, those media provide no immediate record of the communication. In fact, if you were to mention the employee's infraction to the director of human resources over the table during lunch, the director would likely ask you to put it in writing.

Decide Report Design

You can enhance your report-writing efficiency by resolving some aspects of report format before you begin writing. These guidelines can help you successfully format your report.

- *Choose a simple, functional arrangement.* You will impress readers most by providing just the information they need in a way that makes it easy for them to find and understand it. An overly elaborate design may give readers the impression that you did not pay enough attention to the content.
- *Weigh carefully the value of additions such as a glossary of terms.* Add something only if you can justify it on the basis of functionality. For example, if your report contains only a few words that need to be defined, put the definitions in the text. However, if you use many terms that may be unfamiliar to some of your readers, a glossary is a helpful addition. In reports for an international audience, when you cannot avoid using your business terms or jargon, define and explain those terms in the text and in a glossary.
- *Plan for visuals.* While planning your report, look for places where visuals can help explain the points. Instead of giving an array of statistics in your text, turn them into tables and charts.
- *Plan the report format,* including page margins and spacing, font size and style, emphasis techniques, appearance of headings and subheadings, and page numbering. See completed reports on file in your organization or consult a source of report formatting guides, such as *The Gregg Reference Manual.*[6]

- *Know what format decisions you can or may make.* Your company, for example, may already have a standard format for memos, letters, and manuscripts. You may be expected to use certain templates in your word processing software so that documents in a series look alike; or if someone has adapted or created a template for reports like the one you are writing; you may be expected to use it.

Once you identify your purpose, audience, context, and content for a written report; select the report medium; and decide its design, you are ready to outline the report's content. Planning an oral report involves some of these steps and additional ones.

Planning an Oral Report (Presentation)

Effective oral presentations require extensive planning, whether delivered face to face or online. In many ways, preparing an oral report is much like composing a written report. The diagram in Figure 2.4 will guide you through the preparation steps.

- Audience
- Purpose
- Physical environment

- Impromptu
- Extemporaneous
- Scripted
- Memorized
- Combination

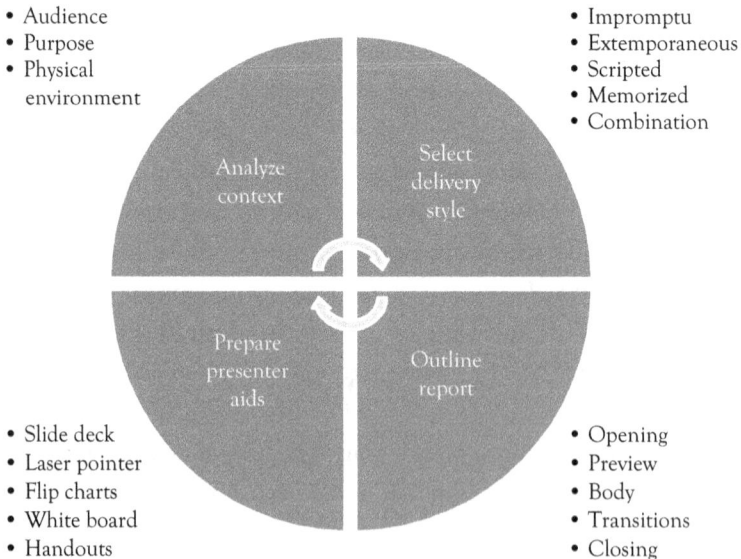

Analyze context

Select delivery style

Prepare presenter aids

Outline report

- Slide deck
- Laser pointer
- Flip charts
- White board
- Handouts

- Opening
- Preview
- Body
- Transitions
- Closing

Figure 2.4 Preparing an Oral Report

Analyze the Context

The communication context encompasses the internal (psychological) environment and the external (physical) environment. Major aspects of context analysis for an oral report, therefore, are determining the characteristics of the intended audience and the characteristics of the place in which you will deliver the presentation. Those two factors tend also to define the appropriate degree of formality.

Audience

Audience analysis is an attempt to assess the psychological environment for the presentation. In this analysis, try to determine who will attend and their motives for attending your presentation. You can expect to give oral reports to four different types of audiences:

- *Clients and customers.* An oral presentation can be a valuable sales technique. Whether you are trying to interest clients in a silicon chip or a bulldozer, you will present its features and its advantages over the competition. Then, after the sale, you will likely narrate to the users detailed operating instructions and maintenance procedures.
- *Colleagues in your organization.* If you are the resident expert on a device, procedure, or technical subject, you will instruct your fellow workers, both technical and nontechnical. After you return from an important conference or an out-of-town project, your supervisors will want a briefing—an oral report. If you have an idea for improving operations at your organization, you probably will write a brief informal proposal and then present the idea orally to a small group of managers. Your presentation will help them determine the advisability of devoting resources to study the idea in greater depth.
- *Fellow professionals at technical meetings or conferences.* As you develop in your profession, you might speak about your own research project or a team project carried out at your organization, or you may be invited to speak to professionals in other

fields—for example, an economist invited to speak to real estate agents about interest rates.

- *The general public.* As you assume greater prominence in your field, you will receive invitations to speak to civic organizations and governmental bodies. Since most organizations encourage employees to participate in community service, you will likely be encouraged to give these presentations.

As you analyze your audience, answer questions such as those listed in Figure 2.5, page 49. Answers to such questions will help you define the psychological environment—how receptive your audience is to your message.

These questions are equally relevant for online and face-to-face presentations. Assume, for example, that you must present the results of your survey of customer preferences for new services at a local bank. An audience of branch managers who know the survey was conducted and are eager to increase business in their respective branches will likely be eager to hear your report. Assume further that the managers will meet immediately after your presentation to make a decision based on your recommendations, one of which is to provide mobile bill payment services. Under those circumstances, the participants will likely listen critically, evaluating every bit of information you present, possibly interrupting with questions and asking for immediate clarification of anything they don't understand. Such an audience would likely be attentive—even late on Friday afternoon! Add to your assumption one manager's opposition to one or more of your recommendations. In such a situation, you should anticipate the need for an especially convincing presentation. You should also expect challenging, perhaps even argumentative, questions from that manager, and you should be prepared with appropriate responses.

Purpose

Consider the purpose of your presentation, just as you would in writing a report. Are you attempting to inform your audience or to both inform and persuade them? If you are explaining how solar power can be used to generate energy, you have one type of argument. If you are explaining why solar power is an economical means of generating power, you have another type.

As you analyze your audience, ask yourself these six questions and write your answers.
1. What is the expected size of the audience?
• Who will attend the presentation?
• What's the name of the group?
• What part of the organization does the audience represent?
• What type of positions do they hold in the company?
• Are the participants predominantly male or mostly female?
• What cultures or ethnicities do they represent?
• How long have they been with the company?
2. Does the audience know much about the topic, or do they know little?
3. What are their reasons for attending the presentation?
• Is the audience part of a problem you will discuss?
• Are participants expected to be part of the solution?
• Are audience members attending voluntarily?
• Are they required to attend?
4. What are their attitudes toward the topic?
• Indifference?
• Opposition?
• Support?
5. What effect will time of the presentation have on participants? Will the audience likely be:
• Alert or drowsy?
• Rested or tired?
6. What are participants expected to do?
• Receive information only?
• Discuss the report?
• Convey information to other employees?
• Participate in a group decision?
• Make a decision at the end of the presentation?
• Make a decision later?
• Make individual decisions?

Figure 2.5 Analyzing a Presentation Audience

Physical Environment

The physical environment also influences the outcome of your presentation. An initially receptive audience can become indifferent or irritable if the physical environment is unsuitable. To define that environment, answer questions such as those listed in Figure 2.6. These questions relate to face-to-face presentations.

1. Where will the face-to-face presentation be made?
• Auditorium?
• Part of a divided hotel ballroom?
• Conference room?
• Classroom?
• Office? Whose office?
2. What furniture arrangement will be used?
• Audience in formal rows facing the speaker?
• Participants and speaker seated at conference table?
• Audience and speaker seated in office with no table?
3. What arrangements must be made for presentation aids? Who will make those arrangements?
4. What presentation aids are possible, and where will they be located in the room?
• Lectern?
• Stationary or mobile microphone?
• Flip chart, marker board, or digital whiteboard?
• Computer hardware?
• Presentation software—specific brand and version?
• Projection equipment and screen?
• Remote control or laser pointer for slide show?
• Electrical outlets?
5. What aspects of the physical environment, if any, may distract from your presentation? Can these potential distractions be removed, controlled, or compensated for?
• Noise?
• Lighting?
• Size of room?
• Kind of seating?
6. What aspects of the environment may you be unable to control? Can you adapt your presentation to accommodate such things?
• Equipment malfunction?
• Power outage?
• Heating, ventilating, and air-conditioning malfunction?
• Insufficient seating?

Figure 2.6 Evaluating the Physical Environment

Knowledge about the physical environment, along with an assessment of the psychological environment, can help you plan your presentation strategies. Consider again your presentation to the bank branch managers. If you want to encourage discussion of your findings, conclusions, and recommendations, you should ask for a conference room arrangement with everyone seated at a table. That arrangement tends to foster discussion more readily than does a formal arrangement with the participants seated in rows facing the speaker. If you anticipate serious discussion of the information, use a handout or a slide show. You may want to consider the following presentation software products:

- Haiku Deck and Haiku Deck Zuru (www.haikudeck.com)
- Keynote for iOS (www.apple.com/ios/keynote) and Keynote 6.6.1 for Macintosh (www.apple.com/mac/keynote)
- Microsoft PowerPoint 2016 (products.office.com)
- SoftMaker's Presentations 2016 (www.softmaker.com)
- Google Presentations (www.google.com/slides/about)
- Prezi (prezi.com)
- Slidebean (slidebean.com)
- Swipe (swipe.to)

Prepare to use available markup options (pen, highlighter, and eraser) in the presentation software. If you want to list or summarize ideas generated during the discussion, be sure you will have access to a document camera, flip chart, or whiteboard (electronic, painted, or virtual), and appropriate writing implements.

For online presentations (webinars), the physical environment is more static than in a face-to-face setting. A typical webinar involves 3 to 15 participants seated at their own computers, equipped with web-conferencing software that permits the participants to interact with the presenter by typing comments and questions and responding to the presenter's on-screen questions. Popular meeting software products include Cisco WebEx, Onstream Webinars, Citrix GoToMeeting 7.6, and GoToWebinar. Guides for preparing a webinar appear in Figure 2.7.

Recognizing the available options in your physical environment can help you achieve success as a speaker. Selecting the appropriate type of delivery can also enhance your oral report.

Take this action	For this reason
Insert your photograph near the beginning of your slide deck. Include your name, organization, and job title if you are not well known to the webinar participants.	This picture will help participants visualize you talking to them during the webinar.
Plan more visuals than you would in a face-to-face presentation. Plan one or two slides per minute when presenting face to face; use about four per minute in a webinar.	In the absence of visuals, audience attention will be more likely to wander since participants cannot focus on you.
On your slides, highlight what you want participants to look at.	Use shading, arrows, and drawing tools available in the software to emphasize details (since you cannot actually point to them).
Omit slides that you would show for only a few seconds.	Some participants may see the slide for only a split second because of a slight lag between advancing the slide and its appearing on the screen. Because of this lag, avoid a sequence of slides or text builds that rely on being synchronized with your spoken words.
Create a special questions slide to display during question-and-answer time.	The slide shown before you pause for questions may be irrelevant—and distracting.
Do the extra rehearsal required.	First, rehearse your presentation until you know it well; then rehearse using the webinar software.

Figure 2.7 Guides for Planning a Webinar[7]

Select the Delivery Style

Five options are available as you select a delivery mode: impromptu, extemporaneous, scripted, memorized, and combination.

Impromptu Delivery Style

Impromptu delivery consists of speaking spontaneously, without previous rehearsal, with little or no advanced preparation and without text or notes to assist you. You will seldom use this type of delivery for the presentation of a major report. You may use it, however, for spontaneous interim progress reports on a project. After you have completed your data collection and analysis for the bank customer survey, for example, your supervisor could ask you in a staff meeting for a quick update on the project. Your presentation in response to that request would be an impromptu speech.

Although impromptu speeches are spontaneous, following these guides will help you make creditable impromptu presentations:

- *Anticipate the major topics that may be discussed.* Play a What if ... game with yourself. Ask, what if I am asked to give an update on the bank customer survey? Answering that question will enable you to consider what information, if any, you will present in the meeting.
- *Avoid being surprised.* Listen attentively; recognize that the discussion is moving into your area of expertise. You can then anticipate that you may be asked for an impromptu statement.
- *Speak for only a minute or two; avoid rambling.* Generally, follow this four-step pattern:
  Step 1 Restate your topic (one sentence).
  Step 2 State one or two key points.
  Step 3 Expand on each point.
  Step 4 Tell listeners what you want them to remember.

Extemporaneous Delivery Style

Extemporaneous delivery appears to be spontaneous but actually involves extensive planning, purposeful rehearsal, and the use of notes during the presentation. With the notes to aid you and the confidence gained during rehearsal, you can establish and maintain eye contact with your audience and move freely about the presentation area. If you have planned and rehearsed your presentation sufficiently, the information will be accurate, complete, organized, and easy to follow. And if you can think well on your feet, the presentation will have a naturalness that will help participants concentrate on what you are saying.

The following suggestions will help you master extemporaneous delivery:

- *Plan every aspect of your presentation*, including the use of visual aids and how you will handle questions.
- *Write your talk*, including notations for visual aids, gestures, audience feedback, and pauses. Read it slowly once or twice to estimate its delivery time. Prepare notes to use during your presentation. Do not memorize your talk.
- *Rehearse the presentation* until it flows smoothly without giving the impression of being memorized. Include your slides and other visuals in the rehearsal, and practice the gestures and moves and pauses you planned. Use your notes only as prompts to keep the presentation flowing smoothly. Time your talk to be sure it fits your allotted presentation time. (In general, the actual talk will take about 25 percent longer than when practicing.) If possible, rehearse before a small audience and ask them to give you feedback.
- *Become thoroughly familiar with the details you want to present.* Understand them; anticipate points that the audience may question.
- *Prepare alternative explanations.* Adapt to audience nonverbal feedback or questions that indicate the participants do not understand some part of the presentation.

You may use extemporaneous delivery in both formal and informal settings. This delivery style is justified when you are very familiar with the information and exact adherence to a prepared script is less important than maintaining eye contact with the audience.

Scripted Delivery Style

Scripted delivery involves reading a manuscript verbatim. This delivery style is appropriate when you are presenting technical or controversial information and you want to ensure that no errors are made in transmission of that information.

Scripted delivery tends to be used in formal more often than informal contexts. Advantages of such delivery are that you can feel confident about the accuracy of your speech and can give an exact copy of your message to members of the audience—preferably after your presentation—to ensure that they receive an accurate message. A disadvantage, however, is that you will have difficulty maintaining eye contact and may miss significant nonverbal reactions from your audience.

To prepare for scripted delivery, follow these guides:

- *Prepare the manuscript* and verify its accuracy.
- *Mark the manuscript with delivery cues*—such as arrows, bold type, and underlining—to indicate pauses and variations in speed or emphasis (and perhaps reminders to smile).
- *Practice reading your manuscript* until you can read it fluently. Avoid reading too quickly.
- *Concentrate on precise enunciation.* Rapid reading frequently leads to slurring or mispronunciation of words.
- *Vary your tone or pitch* to appropriately emphasize the content of your report as you would in conversation.

When the context justifies scripted delivery, be cautious about impromptu discussion following the speech. Although discussion may be appropriate, listen attentively and answer cautiously to avoid contradicting what you said during the delivery.

Memorized Delivery Style

Memorized delivery is presentation of a verbatim message learned by rote. An advantage of memorized delivery is that it allows full freedom of movement and permits you to maintain eye contact with your audience. That delivery style can also promote the audience's confidence in your expertise. A disadvantage, however, is that anxiety may cause you to forget or omit part of the presentation, thereby destroying the coherence of the message and possibly destroying your credibility.

Memorized delivery is appropriate when the volume of information is memorizable and you want to foster participants' confidence in you.

Be cautious, however, about appearing pompous or excessively oratorical. Such an impression tends to alienate an audience.

Combination Delivery Style

Combination delivery employs a variety of delivery styles in a single presentation. You will find this style suitable for many report presentations. In the bank example, for instance, you could deliver a memorized opening statement that will attract attention and stimulate interest in your presentation; that statement could be followed by an extemporaneous presentation of the major findings, conclusions, and recommendations. Perhaps, during the presentation of findings, you may choose to read some statements made by survey participants. And, in answer to a question, you may make an impromptu presentation about further research you think the bank should conduct.

Your analyses of the psychological and the physical environments will also contribute to decisions about the formality of your presentation.

Decide the Formality Level

The decision to give a formal, informal, or semiformal presentation is a practical one. Which formality level will best complement the audience, environment, and topic?

Formal Presentation

In a formal presentation, such as a scripted speech, you will deliver a carefully structured, controlled message with no immediate verbal feedback from the audience. For formal presentations, you will usually stand at a lectern, facing an audience seated in rows. You may use notes or a manuscript to ensure that you proceed through the presentation as planned. You may also use presentation aids—slides, videos, podcast or audio recordings, flip charts, pass-around objects, and handouts—that you have prepared in advance.

A formal presentation leaves little or no room for spontaneous response from the audience; consequently, you must be aware of nonverbal responses to evaluate whether the listeners understand your message. If nonverbal feedback signifies that the audience does not understand or is becoming restless, you should modify your presentation. When appropriate, you may conduct a question-and-answer session after a formal presentation.

Informal Presentation

An informal presentation is also a carefully planned, controlled message, but audience verbal feedback is usually encouraged during the presentation. In an informal presentation, your audience will likely be seated at a conference table or in a semicircle to promote interaction among members of the audience. You may also be seated or standing near the group. You will likely speak extemporaneously, relying on brief notes or presentation aids to direct your talk.

Since members of the audience may ask questions or make comments, an informal presentation can veer from its intended course. To achieve the objective of your report, you must maintain control of the discussion and refocus audience attention on your topic after each question or comment has been given an adequate response.

Semiformal Presentation

In a semiformal presentation, you will strike a middle ground between the formal and informal styles, using a combination style of delivery. In the bank example, for instance, you could give a carefully structured report of your findings as you stand before individuals seated at a conference table, and you might request that they hold their questions until you have presented all findings. Then you could entertain questions about the findings before going on to your conclusions and recommendations. During that part of the presentation, you could sit at the table and permit free discussion of each of the conclusions and recommendations as you present them.

As you plan a presentation, select a degree of formality that complements the topic, the audience, and the physical environment. When the audience is large, a formal presentation may be the most efficient way to present your report. If the findings, conclusions, or recommendations are controversial, you may also choose a formal presentation style so you can present all information before confronting questions. Deferring questions until the end of the presentation may defuse some issues. When the audience is small, a semiformal or informal style may be good, especially if you want to promote discussion. When the audience is a mixed group, with various levels of interest in or knowledge about your topic, a formal presentation may be superior to an informal one. The formal style will permit you to control the presentation more closely and assure that relevant information is presented at a level that is understandable to all members of the audience. For a relatively small, highly motivated, decision-oriented group, an informal style that permits all decision makers to ask questions and evaluate the information is effective.

After choosing a delivery style and formality level appropriate for your audience and context, plan how to supplement your spoken words with presentation aids.

Plan Presentation Aids

Presentation aids are any audio or visual tools you use to supplement your spoken message. A microphone, for example, is an audio tool that can improve your presentation in a large room, enabling everyone to hear you well. A large poster displaying a chart is a visual aid that helps you explain or dramatize data. A slide show illustrates key points and links you to additional aids on the Web, and an audience handout can reinforce your spoken words and promote long-term memory.

Always remember that presentation aids are just that—aids. Adding visuals to a poorly researched, poorly organized oral report will not salvage it. Audio and visual aids should be used to attract and hold attention, clarify meanings, emphasize or elaborate main ideas, or prove a point. Several factors must be considered in selecting the appropriate presentation aid:

- *Constraints of the topic.* Some topics will limit your choice
  of visuals. For example, if you were explaining how a large
  robot operates, you would probably use a video of the robot

in operation. That type of aid could also give the audience cues about the sounds such a robot would make while in operation. A scaled-down model of the robot may not be as valuable since the scope and movement of the machinery may be a persuasive point. Similarly, a drawing or photograph of the robot would be the least effective visual aid.

- *Availability of equipment.* If the presentation site does not have a microphone, you will have to bring your own or be prepared to project your voice to match the needs of the audience. Likewise, if you plan to project a slide show, you must find out whether you need to bring a laptop computer, a digital projector, or speakers for any audio clips in your slide show. And does the presentation site have a projection screen or a white wall you can use for that purpose?

- *Ownership of the presentation aids.* You may find a visual, music, or a sound bite on the Internet that seems ideally suited to support your presentation. Before including it, however, you must determine whether it is in the public domain or subject to copyright laws. Even some visuals on sites such as Google Images are copyright protected. In that case, legal and ethical use requires permission of the copyright holder (owner of the image). Plan ahead when requesting permission from the copyright holder, as getting a reply to your request may take several weeks—or even longer. An e-mail or letter to the owner may be enough to obtain the permission you need. In some instances, permission may be denied, or you may need to pay a fee for use of the image. Permission fees vary widely; you may be able to obtain permission for a few dollars, but in some instances, the permission cost could prohibit use of the presentation aid.

- *Cost of visuals.* Easy access to computers, presentation software, and digital cameras allows for low-cost production of professional visual aids. Still, in some instances, you may be limited to a flip chart or handout. Remember, however, that even inexpensive visuals can be impressive if used purposefully.

- *Difficulty in producing the visual.* If you have only a day or two to prepare for your presentation, it may be impossible to assemble the ideal visual. In a talk about preventing motorcycle theft, for instance, you would like to use a prototype of an antitheft device you invented. If time is short, however, you may need to show drawings instead.
- *Appropriateness of the presentation aid to the audience.* The type of audience and the nature of the presentation affect the choice of audio and visual aids. If you want to use part of a CD, you must be able to select and play the correct tracks without distracting the audience. Some charts, graphs, and diagrams may be too technical for anyone but specialists to grasp. Detailed and complicated tables and charts that require considerable time to digest should be avoided. Generally, the best visuals are simple to use and comprehend.
- *Appropriateness of the presentation aid to the presenter.* Visual aid use requires skill for the desired effect. To use a flip chart, you must be able to speak clearly, write legibly, and draw well-proportioned diagrams. Projected visuals require skill in handling slides and links to videos and websites. If you do not feel comfortable with a particular visual medium, do not use it. Even when you do prepare to use a particular medium, have a backup plan in case something goes awry—such as a presentation file that will not open or a desired website that is temporarily unavailable.
- *Appropriateness of the presentation aid to the time limit.* Carefully check the time required to display and explain a visual to make sure the main ideas of the presentation will not be neglected. Any visual that needs too much explanation is a poor one.

Plan Memorable Visuals

Because we live in a visually oriented society, we expect to see as well as hear information. Therefore, good presenters show as well as tell their points. Two broad categories of visual aids are available to enhance presentations. One category, direct viewing visuals, includes such things as real objects, models, flip charts, diagrams and drawings, photographs, and handouts. The second category, projected visuals, includes slides, videos and DVDs, and websites. Use the following guides to create a slide deck.

- *Choose a design template or theme* provided in the software package or develop your own. Select an appropriate design for the context and appropriate colors for good contrast. Generally, light text on a dark background is preferred. However, if the slides will be printed for a handout, dark text on a light background works best.
- *Avoid using just a few themed templates repeatedly.* You can do this by downloading free templates or themes from sites including the following:
  - o FPPT (www.free-power-point-templates.com)
  - o Google Slides (docs.google.com/presentation/u/0/)
  - o Presentations Pro (www.presentationpro.com/free-sample-powerpoint-templates.aspx)
  - o Slides Carnival (www.slidescarnival.com/category/free-templatesfppt.com)
  - o Smile Templates (www.smiletemplates.com/free/power-point-templates/0.html).
- *Use a readable font size.* Projected text is most readable in size 36 (subpoints) and 32 (supporting information), and no text should be smaller than size 24. Use fonts common to Windows-based computers to avoid possible compatibility problems. Examples include Arial for slide titles and Times New Roman for subtitles and supporting information.
- *Use text sparingly on slides.* To prevent audience overload, follow the 7×7 rule—slides should have no more than five to seven lines per slide and no more than five to seven words per line. About one-fourth of any slide should remain blank.
- *Consider using a text build for bullet lists* that displays only one bullet point at a time as you talk. You may choose to have each line disappear or fade when the next line appears.
- *Consider the Takahaski Technique in lieu of bullet points.* The technique could be called the Keyword Method because each slide in a deck contains only one short, simple word—in huge

letters. Colors and unusual arty fonts give the text a strong visual quality, making points easy to remember.

- *Keep visuals simple.* Each image should focus on one main point. If necessary, prepare several graphics instead of crowding too much information into one exhibit.

- *Use sharply contrasting colors in charts and graphs* to clarify comparisons and relationships.

- *Number all visuals*; mark your notes or manuscript to indicate when each visual will be used.

- *Do not use too many visuals*; each one should add something to the presentation, not detract from it. Generally, the recommended number is one or two slides per minute of your talk.

- *Make each visual large enough* for your audience to see and detect the detail you want noticed.

- *Prepare all visuals in advance and use them in your rehearsal* to help you be confident when using them.

- *Check the room in which you will give your presentation* to be sure it can accommodate your visuals, and check all equipment before the presentation to be sure it is operating properly. Even so, have a backup plan.

Experienced presenters usually create slide decks using a mix of slides with photographs and charts and slides with one word, short phrases, abbreviated sentences, and short quotations. Occasionally in your career, when time is short and your upcoming presentation is exceedingly important, you may opt to hire a presentation design team, such as Haute Slides (hauteslides.com), ProPoint (www.propointgraphics.com), or SlideGenius (www.slidegenius.com) to create your slides. Other groups, such as Duarte (www.duarte.com) and Presentation Partners (www.presentationpartners.com), offer presentation training and help clients plan and organize presentations in addition to designing and producing slide decks.

An additional way to augment your oral reports is to make handouts for the audience. Too often, audience handouts are prepared as an afterthought. To be effective, handouts must be an integral part of oral report planning.

Plan Helpful Handouts

Audience handouts come in two basic forms: a slide printout or expanded notes. Slide printouts—though rarely the ideal handout—are useful for tracking and taking notes on a complex subject and for recalling your message days or weeks later. Audience members can follow up with you using the contact information provided on your handouts.

Rather than printing slides for your whole audience and toting the printouts to your presentation site, post your slides in a shared location you control or use one of the following publicly available sites:

- BackBlaze (www.backblaze.com)
- Dropbox (www.dropbox.com)
- Elephant Drive (www.elephantdrive.com)
- iDrive (www.idrive.com)
- Just Cloud (www.justcloud.com).

Then, a few days before your oral report, notify your audience where the slides are located. If notified in advance, audience members who want a handout can print a copy and bring the materials with them. An alternative is to notify the audience as you begin your oral report, and those interested can print a copy afterward from the shared location. Either practice conserves not only effort and time but also paper and printer ink.

In most instances, a handout should include explanatory text in addition to the slides. If your oral report inspires listeners to want more information about the topic, expanded notes provide that. Expanded notes allow you to simplify your presentation and avoid information overload, because you can refer to the notes while delivering your talk. Thus, expanded notes eliminate concern that you may forget to say some of the details. Creating an expanded notes handout alongside your slide deck involves the software feature called Presenter Notes in Keynote, Speaker's Notes or Notes Pages in PowerPoint, and Presenter View in Prezi. Each page of expanded notes shows a miniature slide, together with explanatory text. The notes can include charts, photographs, and other visuals not included in the slide show.

When creating slides and handouts for your audience, include whatever you believe will aid you in holding audience attention, clarifying meaning, emphasizing ideas, and proving your point. And be willing to edit your slide deck, handout, or both if you make significant changes in your report.

Organizing a Written or Oral Report

The appropriate structure for a report depends on the specific purpose, content, and context of the report. That fact will be demonstrated as you consider nine commonly used structures for entire reports or for parts of reports. These structures also may be applied—in written reports—at the paragraph level.

To help you understand the relationship of report structure to purpose, a specific objective is given in parentheses before each example of structure.

Direct Structure

The direct structure is based on the deductive style of reasoning: from general to specific. A report written in this structure begins with the main point (a generalization), which is followed by supporting data (the facts that justify the generalization). This structure is appropriate when the reader needs little psychological preparation for the main point because it is an expected or easy-to-accept message. The following example demonstrates the direct (deductive) structure. The main point or general statement (Arriving on time ... and we intend to ensure that you do.) precedes the detailed facts about how World Wings has changed flight schedules to and from Atlanta.

Objective: To reinforce customer loyalty

Arriving on time is important to you, and we intend to ensure that you do.

Our goal at World Wings is to deliver fast and reliable service. One of the ways we hope to achieve this is by adjusting flight schedules to and from Atlanta, the world's busiest passenger airport. Beginning

January 31, 2017, our new schedule will offer more than 1,000 daily nonstop flights to nearly 200 domestic and international destinations from Atlanta.

The new schedule will give you:

- More on-time arrivals and departures
- More flight choices
- Less congestion and smoother check-in and security processes

For more information about these changes and other World Wings news, please visit www.worldwings.com.

Thank you for flying World Wings.

Indirect Structure

The indirect structure is based on the inductive style of reasoning, which examines facts and forms generalizations based on those facts. A report written in this structure presents significant data related to the basic purpose of the report, followed by the main point or conclusion supported by those details. This structure is appropriate when the reader requires background details before being able to understand or accept the thrust of the message. The following message demonstrates indirect (inductive) structure. The generalization or conclusion (fewer flights to and from Atlanta) follows the facts that justify the changes.

Objective: To maintain customer loyalty and goodwill in spite of schedule reductions

During 2016, several commercial airlines announced reductions in their flight schedules. Knowing that people who spend much of their time flying with us are key to our success, we at World Wings maintained the number of flights to and from Atlanta, while other carriers were cutting their programs.

To demonstrate our appreciation for your loyalty, we will continue to offer all current early morning and early evening flights. This means you will continue to be able to attend business meetings on a timely schedule and easily make connections with most international flights. Security issues, airport congestion, and spiraling fuel costs, however, require that we curtail the less frequently used flights. Therefore, beginning in 2017, we will reduce the number of flights arriving at and departing from Atlanta between the hours of 10:30 a.m. and 5:30 p.m.

For more information about these changes and other World Wings news, please visit www.worldwings.com.

Thank you for flying World Wings.

Chronological Structure

Chronological structure uses time as the central organizational component of the message. This structure is appropriate when time is an essential ingredient for understanding the basis of a request or for fulfilling that request. Any time units—minutes, hours, days, weeks, months, years, or eras—relevant to the report may be used. The following example illustrates chronological structure.

Objective: To stimulate conference participation and clarify target dates for successful participation

You are invited to participate in the 2018 Association for Human Resource Management Annual Conference. You are especially encouraged to share some of your experience—successful or otherwise—with other human resource managers by presenting a paper or a symposium at the conference in San Luis Potosi, Mexico, on October 20–22, 2018.

Please note these important dates:

April 15, 2018	Deadline for submission of proposal for paper or symposium
April 25, 2018	Acceptance notification
August 1, 2018	Final copy due at Association Headquarters
September 17, 2018	Deadline for conference registration
October 20–22, 2018	Conference in San Luis Potosi, Mexico

The chronological structure may be appropriate for part of a report but not necessarily for the entire report. Chronological structure may also record events by exact time of occurrence; this type of structure is called log structure. The following example illustrates log structure.

Objective: To ensure that convention volunteers fulfill their duties completely and accurately

To ensure that all convention participants have an enjoyable experience, we ask all volunteers to adhere to the following schedule on the first day of the convention, October 20, 2018.

- 6:30 a.m.: Report to Room 398 (Convention Headquarters) in the Hotel Panorama; receive post assignment and all materials needed at that post.
- 7:00 a.m.: Report to post; set up materials.
- 7:30 a.m.: Be prepared to greet visitors to your post.
- 7:30 a.m.–1:00 p.m.: Answer questions posed by visitors; ask each visitor to complete a visitor's survey; report any unusual incidents to R. J. Conway, convention chair, who will be on duty in Room 398.

Please remember: You are the face of AHRM. Please help convention registrants feel welcome when they arrive and be proud of this organization when they leave.

Problem–Solution

As the name implies, the problem–solution structure presents a problem, followed by a proposed solution. This structure works when the problem and proposed solution can be stated concisely and are likely to receive little objection. (Review the first two sections of the e-mail displayed in Figure 1.2 in Chapter 1.) When dealing with a complex problem, you may find the inductive style more fitting because it gives you greater latitude to describe the details of the problem and the reasons for the proposed solution.

Here is an example of the problem–solution structure. Notice how this structure directs the reader's attention to the major elements of the report.

Objective: To stimulate the reader to offer a new amenity to hotel guests

Problem: During the past year, many of our hotel guests have asked whether we have hypoallergenic rooms. Some potential customers have even declined to make a reservation when they were told we do not have such rooms. Our biggest competitor in this area, The Waterfront, has converted one floor to hypoallergenic rooms and has seen its occupancy rate rise 25% over the past year. Meanwhile, our occupancy rate has declined 10% during that time. We appear to be losing some customers because we cannot satisfy their requests for rooms that are free of allergens.

Solution: We should ask Pure Room and EnviroRooms, two companies that specialize in designing allergy-friendly rooms, to give us a bid on converting the fifth floor of our hotel into a hypoallergenic area. The bid should include the costs of retrofitting that floor and a timeline for completing the job. Ideally, we would be able to offer hypoallergenic rooms before we run our fall holiday promotions.

Cause–Effect

When using the cause–effect structure, the writer identifies and discusses conditions (causes) and a predicted outcome (effect) of those conditions. This structure is similar to the inductive one because it moves from specific facts to generalizations based on those facts. The cause–effect structure is appropriate when you want to report your perception of a direct relationship between two or more events. (Review the last two sections of the e-mail in Figure 1.1 in Chapter 1 and the following example of cause–effect structure.)

Objective: To justify an investment in retrofitting hotel rooms to meet hypoallergenic standards

Three months ago, we gave a contract to EnviroRooms to convert the fifth floor of our hotel into a hypoallergenic zone. The work was completed on time and on budget. We are already seeing a return on that investment. The bookings for the Thanksgiving weekend were 10% above last year's bookings. Most of that increase can be attributed to the number of reservations for hypoallergenic rooms.

Spatial Structure

The spatial structure is appropriate any time your data can be presented logically in terms of geographic units. Those units may be as large as continents or nations or as small as areas of a parking lot or a room. You may, for example, wish to analyze the layout of an office, parking lot assignments, productivity by sales districts, or market potential by countries. The spatial structure would be appropriate for the presentation of data analysis, conclusions, or recommendations for each of those reports. The following example demonstrates spatial structure in the presentation of recommendations.

Objective: To meet customer-service needs effectively in all areas of the city

As you requested, I have analyzed customer assistance calls, complaints about customer assistance, and potential needs for customer assistance in our market area. Based on that analysis, I recommend the following changes in service personnel.

Central City	Add one service consultant.
Northeast	Add two service consultants and one technician.
Northwest	Add two service technicians.
Southwest	Reassign one technician from this district to the Southeast district.
Southeast	Assign one technician from the Southwest district and add one service consultant.

Topical Structure

In a topical structure, information is organized around major topics of discussion. A report divided into Findings, Conclusions, and Recommendations is organized topically. To be more meaningful, however, topical headings should identify the factors or elements of analysis. For example, a report presenting the results of a survey to determine preferences for employee benefits could be structured properly in terms of the major categories of benefits, such as medical insurance, retirement plans, child or elder care, and profit sharing. The following example shows headings in a credit union report that was arranged by topic.

Objective: To present credit union performance on major measures of operating success

Subject: Credit Union Performance, 2016

Distribution of Consumer Savings

Text details the distribution of consumer savings among credit union customers. Xxxxx xxxxxxxxx xxxxxxx xxxx xx xxxxxxxx xxx xxxxx. Xxx xxxxx xxxxxxx xx xxx xxxxx. Xxxxx ...

Composition of Savings

Text explains the makeup of savings. Xxx xxxxx xxxxxxx xx xxx xxxxx. Xxxxx xxxxxx xxx xxxxxxx xxxx xx xxxxxxxx xxx xxxxx. Xxx xxxxx xxxxxxx xx xxx xxxxx. Xxxxx xxx xxxx.

Share of Installment Credit Outstanding by Selected Lenders

Text describes the proportion of outstanding installment loans at certain lending institutions. Xxxxx xxxxxx xxx xxxxxxx xxxx xx xxxxxxxx xxx xxxxx. Xxx xxxxx xxxxxxx xx xxx xxxxx.

Share of Auto Loans Outstanding by Selected Lenders

Text states the proportion of outstanding auto loans at specific lending institutions. Xxxx xxxxxxxxx xxx xxxxxxxxxx xx. xxxxxxxxxx xxxxxxxxxxx xxxxx xx xxxxxxx xxxxxxx. Xx-.

Average Loan Rates by Credit Union Asset Size

Text addresses the topic of loan rates in relation to size of the lending institution. Xxxxx xxxxxx xxx xxxxxxx xxxx xx xxxxxxxx xxx xxxxx. Xxx xxxxx xxxxxxx xx xxx xxxxx. Xxx xxxxx xx.

Comparison or Contrast

Comparison or contrast structure examines two or more items in terms of common criteria. Comparison implies examining the qualities of items to discover similarities. Contrasting focuses primarily on differences between or among items.

Assume, for example, that you must prepare a report for college seniors who are thinking of pursuing an MBA degree. The purpose of your report is to provide an objective tool for comparing three MBA programs. You would determine the criteria by which the programs should be evaluated, such as admission standards, cost, availability of financial aid, program requirements, quality of faculty, and placement of graduates. Your report could be structured suitably around those criteria, showing how the programs are similar or different on each criterion. One organizational pattern would evaluate each program on all criteria, as shown in the following example.

Objective: To compare three MBA programs
Program A

- Admission Standards
- Cost
- Financial Aid
- Requirements
- Faculty
- Placement of Graduates

Program B

- Admission Standards
- Cost
- Financial Aid
- Requirements
- Faculty
- Placement of Graduates

Program C

- Admission Standards
- Cost
- Financial Aid
- Requirements
- Faculty
- Placement of Graduates

Another organizational pattern would compare all colleges on each criterion, as shown in the following example.

Admission Standards

- Program A
- Program B
- Program C

Cost

- Program A
- Program B
- Program C

Financial Aid

- Program A
- Program B
- Program C

Requirements

- Program A
- Program B
- Program C

Faculty

- Program A
- Program B
- Program C

Placement of Graduates

- Program A
- Program B
- Program C

Combination Structure

As you may have inferred, few reports adhere to a single structural pattern. The combination structure employs two or more of the patterns discussed. Look again at the example in Figure 1.1. That e-mail uses problem–solution along with cause–effect.

Returning to Case 2.1, assume that you have decided to ask the director to suspend Widener for one day without pay. You could use an inductive structure that begins with a description of the problem and ends with the requested action. Your description of the problem itself could be written in a cause–effect structure, as shown in the following example.

Objective: To ask that Widener be given a one-day suspension
Current problem:
Widener's frequent absence and poor performance on days following her evening job.
History:

- Previous observations of absences and lackluster performance
- Previous corrective action
- Most recent incident

Effects:

- Decline in department morale
- Occasional misuse of sick-leave benefit by other employees

Requested action: Suspend Widener without pay for one day

If you know, however, that the director prefers that reports requesting action begin with the request, your report should be written in the direct structure, and the essential details to support your request could be presented in cause–effect structure.

Requested action: Suspend Widener without pay for one day
Widener's misuse of company sick-leave policy

- History of absences and lackluster performance
- Previous corrective action
- Most recent incident

Effects of Widener's behavior

- Decline in department morale
- Occasional misuse of sick-leave benefit by other employees

An outline will help you plan the structure of your report. The outline should indicate the relative importance of facts and their interrelationships.

Outlining Reports

As you develop your outline—whether it is formal or informal—always keep the reader's or listener's needs uppermost in your mind:

- What does the audience already know about the problem?
- What does the audience look for first?
- What supporting data do the audience need?
- What order of presentation best contributes to audience comprehension of the problem and the solution?
- How will the audience use the information?

Outlining a Written Report

The final outline of your written report reflects your choice of report structure, which, in turn, reflects your understanding of the reader's needs and the purpose for the report.

Informal Outline

An informal outline is a list of topics to be included in the report. It often consists of words, short phrases, or combinations of those elements. Such an outline is primarily an idea-generating tool. For many short reports, the informal outline may be the first and final stage of planning before you draft your report.

Assume, for example, that while eating lunch with the director of human resources, you have mentioned Widener's misuse of the company's sick-leave policy. The director has asked you to send her a brief written report about the situation. A handy way to prepare an informal outline includes three steps.

1. List topics to be included in the report.
   - Widener's part-time job
   - Frequent tardiness or absence after evening work
   - Lackluster performance
   - Other employees' complaints about picking up the slack
   - Rumors that Widener plans to leave
2. Edit the topic list to be sure it contains all essential topics and no unnecessary information. Although the human resources director is the primary reader, your e-mail may become a part of Widener's personnel file. Include all information relevant to the situation—but only that information. Your revised list might look like this:
   - Details about Widener's part-time job: for whom she works, when she works, how long she has worked there
   - Records of tardiness or absences
   - Previous discussions with Widener: when, where, summary of discussion
   - No change in behavior
   - Request suspension
3. Arrange topics in a sequence that shows relationships of key points and satisfies the communication needs of your readers. Since the human resources director is a busy person who already knows something about Widener's infraction, you may decide to use the direct structure.
   - Request that Widener be suspended one day without pay
   - Details about Widener's part-time job
   - Summary of Widener's tardiness and absences
   - Previous discussions with Widener
   - Results of discussions with Widener

An informal outline will readily communicate necessary information to you as the writer and will help you compile your report with ease. For a complex situation, however, you may be dealing with a considerable amount of information and an extensive analysis of that data. To help you produce a coherent, well-organized report in that case, you would do well to prepare a formal outline.

Formal Outline

A formal outline is a useful communication tool both before and as you write the report. If you wish to discuss the content and structure of your report with a supervisor or a colleague before you begin writing, you can use the outline as a guide. If you follow the outline faithfully while writing the report, you will be sure to cover all essential data.

A formal outline employs a structured numbering system to show the various levels into which the report is divided. Phrases or sentences are used to describe the content of each division and subdivision of the report. Depending largely on the preferences of your report readers, you may use either the traditional outline system or a decimal system to number the sections.

The traditional outline system consists of Roman numerals to indicate first-level divisions, uppercase letters for second-level divisions, Arabic numerals for third-level divisions, and lowercase letters for fourth-level divisions. Few outlines progress beyond fourth-level divisions; but when you need such divisions, continue the numbering system by alternating Arabic numerals and lowercase letters. The *Chicago Manual of Style*[8] recommends that the divisional numerals or letters for the first three levels be set off by periods and that those used for the lower levels be set off by single or double parentheses. The manual also gives the sage advice that what is most important in the development of an outline and its numbering system is that the reader be able to see at a glance the level to which each item belongs.

To illustrate the preparation of a formal outline using the traditional system, assume the following facts.

Context: Your company, BestMeters, specializes in the manufacture and service of flowmeters, which are used in many industries that transport a liquid product and must measure the flow of that product during delivery.

Situation: The company wishes to expand its business by marketing its BESTFLO meter in the South American market. This meter is an electronic unit that is mounted on a truck and measures the flow of liquefied petroleum gas (LPG) at the point of delivery. Preliminary research has shown that demand for the product would likely be strongest in Argentina, Brazil, and Venezuela. However, management needs extensive information about the nature of the market before deciding whether to launch a South American venture.

Report Objective: You were asked to evaluate the potential market for the BESTFLO meter in Argentina, Brazil, and Venezuela. Specifically, you attempted to answer four questions for each of the three countries:

1. What economic conditions influence the development of the LPG industry?
2. What is the general sales potential for BESTFLO?
3. Who are the primary customers and the largest companies distributing LPG?
4. What are the optimal means of distributing and promoting BESTFLO?

Status: You have completed your research and are about to write the report.

Primary Audience: Your report will be presented to the vice president for marketing, Robert Montero. Mr. Montero is familiar with the purpose of the research, and he discussed it at length when he authorized you to conduct the study. You gave him periodic progress reports as you worked on the project. He is eager to learn your findings, conclusions, and recommendations and would be satisfied with an informal outline and an oral report.

Secondary Audience: Mr. Montero will present your report to the executive committee. He wants you to include full background information and details about how you conducted your study so that all members of the committee can understand the situation fully.

A formal outline such as the one shown in Figure 2.8 would guide your discussion with Mr. Montero and help you prepare an effective written report for the executive committee.

Feasibility of Marketing BESTFLO in South America
I.   Background: BestMeters wants to expand its market for BESTFLO.

II. Research Question: Is it feasible to promote BESTFLO to the South American LPG industry?
A. Purpose of the study
B. Scope of analysis
C. Method of study
   1. Data sources
   2. Data collection
   3. Data analysis

III. Findings
A. Economic conditions
   1. Argentina
   2. Brazil
   3. Venezuela
B. Sales potential for LPG flowmeters
   1. Argentina
   2. Brazil
   3. Venezuela
C. Primary competitors
   1. Argentina
   2. Brazil
   3. Venezuela
D. Distribution and promotion strategies

IV. Conclusions A. Growing market for flowmeters in the three countries B. LPG distribution controlled by few companies C. Few competitors in the market D. Unique characteristics of each country require country-specific adaptations

V. Recommendations
A. Respond quickly to growing market
B. Establish BESTFLO as industry standard
   1. Adapt meter for needs of specific countries
   2. Target nine specific LPG suppliers
C. Educate potential customers
   1. Quality of BESTFLO
   2. Competitive price of BESTFLO

Figure 2.8 Traditional Outline

The decimal system, used by many engineering companies, law firms, and government agencies, uses Arabic numerals and decimals to indicate main topics and subtopics. The numbering begins with a single digit (1, 2, 3, etc.) to mark first-level divisions. For each subdivision, a decimal is added and the parts of that subdivision are numbered consecutively (1.1, 1.2; 2.1, 2.2; 2.2.1, 2.2.2, etc.).

Figure 2.9 shows the decimal system of outlining. You can check the accuracy of your decimal numbering system by comparing the numbers with the division level. Notice that every first-level division is marked with a single number; every second-level division has two numbers, separated by a decimal; every third-level division has three numbers, separated by decimals; and so on.

Both systems, traditional and decimal, require that you observe basic outlining guidelines.

Improving Organizational Effectiveness
1. Define organizational mission

2. Identify organizational goals
  2.1 Unit goals
    2.1.1 Short term
    2.1.2 Long term
  2.2 Department goals
    2.2.1 Short term
    2.2.2 Long term
  2.3 Division goals
    2.3.1 Short term
    2.3.2 Long term
  2.4 Organization goals
    2.4.1 Short term
    2.4.2 Long term

3. Determine performance criteria
  3.1 Unit level
  3.2 Department level
  3.3 Division level
  3.4 Organization level

4. Assess organizational effectiveness
  4.1 Select indicators
  4.2 Select samples
  4.3 Collect data
  4.4 Apply criteria
  4.5 Interpret findings

5. Use assessment findings
  5.1 Identify strengths and weaknesses
  5.2 Modify goals
  5.3 Allocate resources

Figure 2.9 Decimal Outline

Outlining Guidelines

To communicate report content well, your outline must be clear and coherent. Observing the following guides will help you achieve those qualities.

- *Every division and subdivision must have at least two parts.* Logically, nothing can be divided into less than two parts. Therefore, every topic that is divided must have a minimum of two subtopics. The following examples contrast ineffective, illogical outline divisions with effective, logical divisions.

Illogical; Ineffective	Logical; Effective
A. The current system	A. The current system
1. Inefficient	1. Inefficient
	2. Error prone
	3. Costly
B. The proposed system	B. The proposed system
1. Efficient	1. Efficient
	2. Accurate
	3. Cost-effective

- *Divisions should be balanced.* All divisions need not have the same number of topics and subtopics; but if any section of your outline is considerably longer or shorter than other sections, you should reevaluate the outline. Lack of balance may suggest the need to regroup information for a more coherent report structure. The following examples contrast unbalanced, ineffective sections with balanced, effective sections.

Unbalanced; Ineffective	Balanced; Effective
A. The current system	A. The current system
1. Inefficient	1. Inefficient
	2. Error prone
	3. Costly

B. The proposed system	B. The proposed system
1. Easily learned	1. Efficient
2. Fast	2. Accurate
3. Accurate	3. Cost-effective
4. Desired by employees	
5. Easy to correct errors	
6. Inexpensive to install	
7. Inexpensive to operate	
8. Can use some of old equipment	

- *Divisions and subdivisions should help readers focus quickly* on significant report content. When any part of an outline contains more than four division levels, you may be focusing the reader's attention on minor rather than major points. The following examples show how the previous outlines can be improved by clarifying major and minor points.

Major and Minor Points Unclear	**Major and Minor Points Clear**
The proposed system:	The proposed system:
Easily learned	Efficient
Fast	Fast
Accurate	Accurate
Desired by employees	Easy corrections
Easy to correct errors	Cost-effective
Inexpensive to install	Inexpensive to install
Inexpensive to operate	Inexpensive to operate
Can use some of old equipment	Use some old equipment
	Acceptable to employees
	Desired
	Easily learned

- *Division headings should be stated concisely.* Topic headings, such as those often used in a tentative outline, may be too concise to communicate report content to the reader. If the outline in Figure 2.9 were a topic outline, the first-level headings might be single words or short phases, such as mission, goals, criteria, assessment, and use. Although such an outline may guide the report writer, it conveys little to the readers.

Talking headings, written in parallel phrases or short sentences as in Figure 2.9, provide more information about the report content. Lengthy talking headings, however, may distract from communication. Assume, for example, that Heading 2 was written in this way: *Identify goals by getting input at all organizational levels.* Such a heading burdens the reader with unnecessary words, particularly since the subtopics listed under the heading indicate that goals must be identified at all levels.

- *Division topics must be expressed in parallel grammatical structure.* Appropriate parallelism is demonstrated in Figure 2.9. Notice that first-level divisions (1 through 5) are grammatically parallel; second-level divisions, such as 2.1 through 2.4, are parallel within the division but not necessarily parallel with other second-level divisions, such as 4.1 through 4.5.

- *Special timesaving tools in most word processing software help you create and reorganize outlines*, as well as evaluate the organization of a finished report. In Microsoft Word 2016, for example, both the multilevel-list tool and the outline view are designed to facilitate outlining. Outline view is the more versatile of the two, in that you can quickly change the level and order of topics, as well as reduce visual clutter by hiding selected parts of an outline.

The final outline of your report reflects your choice of report structure, which in turn reflects your understanding of the reader's needs and the report's purpose.

Outlining a Presentation (Oral Report)

A simple yet helpful outline structure for an oral report consists of four parts: the opening, a preview or partition statement, the body, and the conclusion. Each must be worded to formulate a coherent presentation that accomplishes your reporting purpose, and the parts must be connected by meaningful transitions. In addition, any presentation aids you will use must be planned from your presentation outline.

As you prepare a talk, maintain a thorough outline of every element you want to include. Organize your outline along the lines presented in Figure 2.10.

Presentation title:	B. Main point 2
	1. Subpoint 1
	a. Supporting information
	b. Supporting information
Presenter's purpose:	2. Subpoint 2
	a. Supporting information
I. Introduction	b. Supporting information
A. Strong attention-getting opener	C. Main point 3
B. Topic of presentation	1. Subpoint 1
C. Relevance of topic	a. Supporting information
D. Preview or partition statement	b. Supporting information
	c. Supporting information
II. Body	2. Subpoint 2
A. Main point 1	a. Supporting information
1. Subpoint 1	b. Supporting information
a. Supporting information	c. Supporting information
b. Supporting information	
2. Subpoint 2	III. Conclusion
a. Supporting information	A. Summary of main points
b. Supporting information	B. Relationship of main point(s) to presenter's purpose
	C. Memorable closing statement

Figure 2.10 Oral Report Outline

Strong Opening

The opening of your talk must reach out and grab the listeners' attention. A good opening draws the audience into the message by showing its relevance to them. Such an opening focuses on the audience, not on the speaker. Some effective attention-getting openings are quotations, surprising statements, questions, stories, or relevant statistics.

Some speakers have the mistaken idea that all speeches should begin with a joke. A humorous opening is appropriate only if the humor relates to the speech topic, offends no one in the audience, and is delivered skillfully.

Compare the following examples of ineffective and effective opening statements.

Ineffective: Today I'm going to give you the results of the survey of Midland National Bank customers that Mr. Hector asked me to conduct last month. I think you might be interested in some of the results. [Focuses on speaker; tentatively suggests topic may be relevant to listeners.]

Effective: Your customers want innovative bank services that will give them easier access to their accounts. You can give them those services at very little extra cost to your branch. [Focuses on listeners; establishes relevance of message to them.]

Ineffective: What's the slowest-moving line in the world? The line at the teller's window I just chose. I always manage to choose the slowest-moving line. Seriously, folks, I'm here to tell you about your recent customer survey and what it suggests about service at your bank. [Trite joke that may offend audience members; focuses on speaker; doesn't recognize participants' needs.]

Effective: Eighty percent of your banking customers are satisfied with Midland services. That's good news. Today I'd like to suggest how you can turn good news into even better news—how satisfied customers can become extremely satisfied customers. [Pleasing statistic involving the audience; shows immediate relevance of the talk to participants.]

Meaningful Preview Statement

The preview (partition) statement tells the audience what your talk will cover. This statement should create a mental readiness or map that will help the listeners follow your presentation. A partition statement should identify clearly and interestingly the topics to be covered so that participants can anticipate the message that unfolds. Compare the following examples of effective and ineffective partition statements.

Ineffective: As I said, Mr. Hector asked me to find out what Midland National Bank customers think about some services that we are considering for our customers. So I basically asked them about five different services. In this presentation I'm going to tell you what those services are, how customers responded to the survey, and some recommendations based on their responses. [Continues to focus on speaker; gives no clue about specific content of message or relevance to audience; provides only a structural overview: questions asked, responses, recommendations.]

Effective: My recommendation will be based on two major findings from our study of Midland National Bank (MNB) customer attitudes toward proposed new banking services. MNB customers showed the strongest interest in new services that give them easy access to their accounts. They showed little interest in incentives for some of our standard consumer banking services. Today I'd like to share with you what we found out about consumer preferences, specifically the services they expressed interest in and the services they were indifferent to. I'll also make some recommendations about how we can satisfy MNB customer preferences. [Heightens interest; tells what will be covered; creates a receptive frame of mind because it suggests relevance to audience.]

Well-Developed Main Points

The body of the presentation must adequately develop the points identified in the preview statement. An appropriate sequence of information following the previous effective preview statement would be (1) services preferred by customers, (2) services about which customers were indifferent, and (3) recommendations for providing the preferred services.

Development can be achieved by presenting statistics, examples of customer comments, costs of implementing certain services, and any additional data that will support your recommendations and enable listeners to reach an effective decision.

Engaging Language

If people doze off while reading a report you have written, you probably will not know it, at least not until they complain to you later or you realize that the report failed to accomplish its purpose. But if they doze off while you are speaking to them, you will know it right away. Engaging presentations require memorable language.

To help make your language memorable, use these three techniques:

- *Involve the audience.* People are more interested in their own concerns than in yours. Talk to the audience about their problems and their solutions. In the introduction, establish a link between your topic and the participants' interests. For instance, in a presentation to the Gafney City Council about waste management, you might begin like this: Picture yourself on the Gafney City Council two years from now. After exhaustive hearings, proposals, and feasibility studies, you still do not have a waste-management plan that meets federal regulations. What you do have is a mounting debt, as the city is assessed $1,000 a day until you implement an acceptable plan.
- *Refer to people, not to abstractions.* People remember specifics; they forget abstractions. When you want to make a point memorable, describe it in human terms. What could you do with that $365,000 every year? You could buy almost 400 computers; that's a computer for almost every classroom in every elementary school in Arcadia Township. You could expand your school-lunch program to feed every needy child in the township. You could extend your after-school programs to cover an additional 3,000 students.
- *Use interesting facts, figures, and quotations.* Do your research and find interesting information about your subject. For

instance, you might find a brief quotation from an authoritative figure in the field (Tim Cook on cell phone security?) or a famous person not generally associated with the field (Mark Zuckerberg on poverty and hunger?).

Purposeful Transitions

Ideas within your presentation must be linked logically and clearly. Transitional words or phrases help the audience understand a discussion by pointing out the direction of the presentation. All parts of the presentation should be linked together by simple transitions that demonstrate the organizational pattern you are using. The introductory preview acts as a transition to the body of the presentation. When you move from one main point to another, use a statement announcing the move: Now that we have looked at _____, let's look at _____.

Likewise, you should announce demonstrations, examples, digressions, or comparisons and contrasts when they occur: An example of _____ occurs when.... Finally, make a clear transition when you begin the conclusion of the presentation: Now that we have discussed each of the three main points, let's summarize the key elements.

Weak speakers often overlook these simple transitional sentences, but transitions can be one of your best tactics to help the audience follow your points. Because participants do not have the outline of the presentation in front of them, you must verbalize the structure of the outline to keep them on track. Here are several other transition clauses you may find helpful for unifying your presentation.

Enumeration:	My first point is ...
Importance:	A more important fact is ...
Emphasis:	The main point to remember is ...
Addition:	Another thing to consider is ...
Tangents:	This is off the subject, but ...
Return:	Let me get back to where I was.
Leading:	The next thing to look at is ...
Question:	What is the next thing to consider?

Preview:	I will deal with three main ideas.
Internal:	Let me conclude this section.
Summary:	Let me repeat my main ideas.

Consider the following examples of ineffective and effective transitions.

Ineffective: So that's pretty much what customers thought about services that give them easier access to their accounts. Now let's look at their evaluations of some other kinds of services. [Does not summarize the completed part; provides no clue about content of the next part; gives no indication of how the two parts are related.]

Effective: As you have seen, our customers gave "important" or "very important" ratings to the two mobile services related to accessing accounts: an application that allows customers to make deposits using their smartphones and cardless ATMs from which customers can withdraw currency using their phones. In contrast, MNB customers showed little interest in additional ATM locations, Saturday morning teller service, or even additional online banking services. [Summarizes one part of presentation; links it to the next part of presentation.]

Memorable Conclusion

The conclusion should clinch the message; that is, it should be what you want the listeners to take away. For an informative talk, the conclusion must help the listeners remember the main points of the message. For a persuasive presentation, the conclusion should stimulate action based on the message. Be sure to link the conclusion to the body of the talk by a meaningful transition.

Good ways to end a presentation include summaries of the report content, requests or proposals for specific actions, examples or anecdotes that reinforce the message, questions that prompt a response or action, or combinations of those strategies. The closing should be a memorable finish for the audience, not a letdown or abrupt stop. Compare the following examples of effective and ineffective conclusions.

Ineffective: That's about all I found out. Based on the findings, it looks like it might be a good idea to provide more mobile phone options. [Does not summarize or recap the report; tentatively hints at action.]

Effective: Evidence indicates that MNB customers want more mobile banking services than we currently provide. The simplest, least costly way to give them those services is to provide a mobile deposit application, such as Deposit@Mobile; and install cardless ATMs, such as NCR Mobile Cash Withdrawal. Three local competitors currently offer mobile deposits, but none offers cardless ATMs. I recommend that we initiate mobile deposits by December 1 and mobile withdrawals by March 1 next year. Doing so will demonstrate to our current customers—and also to some potential ones—that MNB believes in service. [Summarizes major findings; confidently proposes a specific action and the likely outcome of that action.]

Outlines vary tremendously because you must adapt them to the situation and the purpose of the presentation. Whatever the case, take care to organize clearly. Use a framework that allows you to see at a glance how the presentation is structured. A good outline will help you stay organized as you speak, adjust the presentation to time constraints, add or subtract material, and find your place if you become lost during the talk. Prepare your outline using complete sentences, partial sentences, key phrases, or key words. Experiment with various forms of outlines until you find one that is particularly useful to you.

Most of you have prepared both written and oral reports through collaboration—two or more people working together to create a final product. As you progress in your career, it will become increasingly important for you to work effectively on team projects.

Planning Team Reports

Understanding how teams form and develop may help you function effectively as a team participant or leader. In addition, following the advice of experienced collaborators will help you contribute significantly to team projects.

Planning a Team Written Report

Early planning efforts for a team project typically focus on group processes first and then task requirements. Once the team members have been notified of the task, they must first form a team as opposed to a mere collection of people. Only after team formation can the group members actually move on to planning and eventually producing the report. Group members must become acquainted with one another and identify individuals' strengths, weaknesses, work styles, and so on.

Forming a Team

Tuckman's classic 1965 study on group formation identified four stages of group development: forming, storming, norming, and performing. A fifth stage, adjourning, was added later.[9]

- *Forming.* The forming stage is also called the orientation stage. During this stage, a team becomes oriented to the task, sets initial goals, and begins to establish ground rules. And a team leader may begin to emerge during this stage because members will look to someone for guidance. Team members act courteously toward one another as they become acquainted and test the waters to determine just how the group will operate.
- *Storming.* The storming stage is marked by conflict among team members. The group is typically eager to proceed with the task, but disagreements may arise about goals and procedures. Conflicts can lead to resentments and the development of subgroups. Dysfunctional behaviors (blocking, dominating, competing, withdrawing, and repeating) often characterize this stage.

  The storming stage can be productive, however, if it teaches team members how to deal with their differences. The storming phase can bring out the creativity of team members if they are willing to consider all proposals. Effective teams capture the energy generated at this stage and direct it positively. Constructive task-oriented behaviors (initiating discussion, seeking information, giving information, coordinating comments, evaluating suggestions, and summarizing) will help the group keep on task. And process-oriented behaviors (encouraging participation, harmonizing differing viewpoints, opening gates to people who are attempting to join the discussion, and setting standards) will foster greater team unity.

- *Norming.* If the team successfully navigates the storming phase, it moves into norming. Typical characteristics of the norming phase include openness to other team members, cooperation, and mutual support. The team becomes more focused on the task, and the members become aware of themselves as a functioning organization with a common goal and team spirit.

  Because of the strong focus on task, the threat of "groupthink" exists at this stage. Wanting to move forward, members may hesitate to challenge the prevailing direction of the team. It is especially important that members use their process-oriented skills to encourage all ideas to come forward.

- *Performing.* In the performing stage, task-oriented behaviors characterize the interactions among team members, who are generally able to work harmoniously toward achieving their common goal. In this stage, the team functions as a relatively cohesive work unit, with a minimum of emotional interference. Typically, team members can function individually or in any combination with other members on parts of the task because goals and standards have been set. Questions still arise, but the team members are able to harmonize differences by practicing their process-oriented skills.

- *Adjourning.* Having completed the task, successful teams pass purposefully through the adjourning stage. At this stage, members often feel exhilaration due to successful accomplishment of a task and sadness or anxiety that the team will disband—and perhaps never again work together. Successful teams evaluate what has occurred in terms of their task accomplishment and their skill development. This phase is an opportunity to appreciate what has been done well, recognize what might have been done better, and acknowledge the behaviors that contributed to successes or failures. Members can then apply that knowledge as they approach a new team project.

For more information about Tuckman's team development model, refer to ess110.files.wordpress.com/2009/02/tuckmans_model.pdf.

Awareness of the team developmental stages by all members increases the likelihood of successful collaboration. As the model implies, collaboration involves empathy, consideration, group loyalty, and other traits, as cited in the following team guidelines.

- *Have empathy for the other collaborators.* See their point of view. Do not assume that you know what they are saying or are going to say. Actively listen to what they are saying.
- *Be considerate of others.* Support the other members of the group with compliments and friendliness. Be supportive by using motivation rather than pressure to inspire people to act.
- *Be loyal to the group without agreeing with everything.* Tactfully assert yourself when you have a contribution to make or when you disagree.
- *Invite criticism of your contributions and be ready to criticize your own ideas.* Detach yourself from your ideas and try to see them objectively, as you hope others will.
- *Never attack people personally for their ideas.* The criticism should be directed at the idea, not at the person.
- *Understand that communication often breaks down.* Do not be shocked when you are misunderstood or when you misunderstand others.
- *Remember that most ideas that are not obvious seem strange at first*, yet they may be the best ideas of all.

Reviewing these planning guides each time you begin a collaborative project will get you off to a productive start and help bring you to a satisfying end of the project.

Writing Collaboratively

A team report should be seamless; readers should not be able to tell where one person's work leaves off and another's begins. In reality, collaborative writing often consists of a combination of collective and independent work, depending on the stage of the project.

During the planning phase, the writing team should collectively identify the audience, purpose, and scope of the project. At this point, the team should review the overall project to be sure everyone understands the expected outcome. After the scope of the project has been identified, the team may assign specific responsibilities to individual team members.

The team may also develop a preliminary outline for the final report to ensure that all necessary topics are covered and to guide the team members as they gather data, analyze, and write. Naturally, the team members must always allow for revisions in their outline as new perspectives arise during the data collection and analysis stages of the report.

In addition, the team should discuss possible sources of both primary and secondary data for their report. For a report that will involve a large amount of secondary (published) data, team members might compile an annotated bibliography; that is, a list of print and web publications with appropriate comments about each entry. Then, during the data collection stage, individuals can refer to this list for help in locating relevant data.

Another collective task during the planning period is to agree on a general writing style, formal or informal. The team should also make formatting decisions or select a standard template so that all writers use the same software for their drafts; within that software, each should use the agreed-on margins, font, typeface, type size, and type style for the report body and headings. These formatting decisions will ease the process of merging individuals' writing into a single, unified report. These days, teams often create and edit reports using inexpensive or free online software, such as Google Docs—www.google.com. Using Google Docs or similar software, all team members can add and review report content and type comments about it—as the report is being written.

Oral reports are often developed from a team's written report and delivered by the team of presenters—especially if the presentation requires the input of people with different expertise. For example, individuals from accounting, marketing, and human resources all may be involved in a team presentation regarding the creation of a team to manage a new business account.

Planning a Team Oral Report (Presentation)

A team oral report should be a carefully arranged performance that gives the impression of a single, unified report rather than a series of individual talks. The following planning guides will help you achieve coherent team presentations:

- *As the report is prepared, individuals should be given responsibility for specific parts of the presentation.* Ideally, each person will assume primary responsibility for a part about which he or she is most knowledgeable.
- *All members of the team should be familiar with the total report,* not only with the parts for which they have primary responsibility.
- *Inexperienced teams should plan for a distributed (divided) presentation format.* In it, team members divide topics in their report outline, one to each person. More experienced teams may accept the challenge of a merged (integrated) presentation format. In it, team members collaborate on a very detailed outline of points and examples; then they take turns presenting within each point. Merged format helps keep the listeners' interest, but it works only when (1) all team members know the subject well and (2) the group is willing and able to rehearse extensively.
- *One team member should serve as the coordinator.* This individual will introduce the presentation, the team members, and their respective topics, and will direct the talk or presenters. The coordinator may also be responsible for summarizing the report and moderating the question-and-answer session.

Summary

As you plan, organize, and outline your reports, the following checklists can help keep you on track.

When planning a written report, complete the following items. Also, make notes as you go that you can refer to for organizing and outlining and then for drafting, revising, and producing your report.

Written Report Planning Checklist

- ☐ *Identify your purpose.* What is your general purpose: production (most often), innovation, or goodwill? Then, specifically, what do you want the receiver(s) of your report to do?
- ☐ *Identify your audience, both primary and secondary.* Noting peoples' names or job titles is not enough. Ask yourself what information the receivers will need. Also question whether the receivers—the primary audience in particular—are likely to have objections that you must try to overcome.
- ☐ *Identify the context.* Think about overall circumstances. And try to offset any physical or psychological conditions that could keep your report from achieving its purpose.
- ☐ *Identify report content.* On the basis of purpose, audience, and context, identify what information to include—and exclude—in your report.
- ☐ *Select a medium.* Remember, some means of transmitting a report are rich, while others are lean. As a general rule, use lean media for reporting about routine management situations. Use richer media for nonroutine issues.
- ☐ *Adopt a design for the report.* Choose a simple arrangement, adding special parts—such as an appendix or a glossary— as audience needs dictate. Plan where to insert visuals to increase effectiveness; and take time upfront to choose fonts, headings, margins, page numbering, and spacing.

Oral Report Planning Checklist

☐ *Analyze the context,* including your audience, purpose, and physical environment. Use Figures 2.5 and 2.6 to guide analysis of audience and physical environment.

☐ *Choose a suitable delivery style*—extemporaneous, impromptu, memorized, or scripted. Most experienced presenters use a combination of these delivery styles.

☐ *Decide the formality level:* formal, informal, or semi-formal. In general, choose formal when presenting to a large audience and informal when talking to a few people. Sometimes a combination of formality levels may be appropriate during your oral report.

☐ *Select presentation aids to enhance your spoken message.* Consider availability, cost, and time constraints in particular. Be aware that today's audiences will expect you to use visual enhancements. Remember also that audience handouts can reinforce and extend your oral report.

Before organizing a report, review your notes about your purpose, audience, context, and so on. Choose from the following report structures, matching the structure to your context, audience, and specific purpose.

Report Organization Checklist

☐ *Direct (deductive structure) presents the main message first, followed by details.* Use this structure when report readers will find the report easy to understand and the outcomes easy to accept.

☐ *Indirect (inductive) structure gives detailed information; then, generalizes from those facts.* This structure is recommended when readers need background information to understand, accept the gist of your report, or both.

☐ *Chronological structure uses time units as the way of organizing the report.* Use this structure when time is essential to understanding the report and the subsequent action to be taken.

☐ *Problem–solution structure involves a stated problem followed by a proposed solution.* Use this structure under these conditions: the problem and your solution can be stated concisely. Otherwise, use indirect structure instead.

☐ *Cause–effect structure is similar to indirect structure; both move from specifics to generalities.* Use this structure when you want to emphasize an apparent relationship between two conditions or events.

☐ *Spatial structure presents data in geographical terms*—units as large as continents or as small as sections of a conference room. Use it whenever your data can be presented logically in geographical units.

☐ *Topical structure organizes reports by major discussion topics.* Use topical structure when none of the foregoing structures seems appropriate. Be sure to use topic headings that identify what factors you studied.

☐ *Comparison or contrast structure uses a single set of criteria to study two or more items.* Comparison observes items for similarities, while contrast looks for differences.

☐ *Combination structure involves two or more structures on this list.* In this book, examples demonstrate a combination of cause–effect and problem–solution as well as indirect structure and cause–effect.

In a report outline, you implement your plan and your structure choice. For a written report, your outline may be informal (list of keywords, phrases, or both) or formal (structured numbering system), depending on the report's scope and complexity. A formal outline may be traditional (first-level divisions labeled with Roman numerals, second-level with capital letters, and third-level with Arabic numbers) or decimal (first-level divisions labeled with Arabic numbers [1, 2, 3, etc.], second level with decimal numbers [1.1, 1.2, etc.], and third level with an additional decimal and number [1.1.1, 1.2.1, etc.]). Decimal outlines are the typical choice in engineering, law, and government offices.

If you create a formal outline for your written reports, check that every divided topic has two or more subtopics; outline divisions are rather balanced; the outline includes no more than four levels; division headings are concise, informative (talking) phrases, or abbreviated sentences; and division headings at a given level are in the same grammatical form (parallel).

Put four main divisions in your oral report outlines.

Presentation Outline Checklist

☐ *Strong opening.* Start your presentation (oral report) outline with a means for getting audience attention and showing relevance of your report to them. Include a meaningful preview statement that states the main topics you will cover, which will help the audience follow your oral report.

☐ *Well-developed main points.* Taking each topic in turn, list details that will support your purpose and help your audience take appropriate action.

☐ *Purposeful transitions.* Jot down how you will signal each topic change for the audience.

☐ *Memorable conclusion.* Write out the one idea you want your audience to remember above all others.

When collaborating with a team to create a written or oral report, keep in mind that teams develop in stages generally recognized as forming, storming, norming, performing, and adjourning. Making everyone on the team aware of these stages and practicing empathy, consideration, and team loyalty will increase the team's chances of turning out a seamless report.

CHAPTER 3

Planning Research

Managers must often make decisions that will have a major impact on the success of their organizations. Should a would-be entrepreneur begin the business he has long contemplated? Should an automobile manufacturer discontinue a product line? Should an advertising agency give a substantial amount of money to a state university to establish a business communication center? Should an insurance company change its policy about medical insurance coverage for domestic partners? These and other questions require extensive research before they can be answered with confidence.

The first step in the research process is to create a plan that clearly identifies the problem to be studied and its scope as well as the purpose of the study and the audience to whom the information will be reported. All factors related to the study, including costs and time required, may be presented formally in a research proposal.

Making a Research Plan

A report about a complex problem begins with a research plan, which becomes a guide for collecting data, analyzing data, and reporting the results of the analysis.

A research plan, as indicated in Figure 3.1, includes 12 parts: obtain or review authorization, identify the audience, define the problem, clarify the purpose, narrow the scope, state delimitations and limitations, plan data collection, plan data analysis, estimate time schedule, estimate resources needed, plan the presentation of results, and seek approval to proceed.

Obtain or review authorization
↓
Identify the audience*
↑↓
Define the problem*
↑↓
Clarify the purpose*
↑↓
Narrow the scope*
↑↓
State delimitations and limitations*
↑↓
Plan data collection
↓
Plan data analysis
↓
Estimate time schedule
↓
Estimate resources needed
↓
Plan presentation of results
↓
Seek approval to proceed

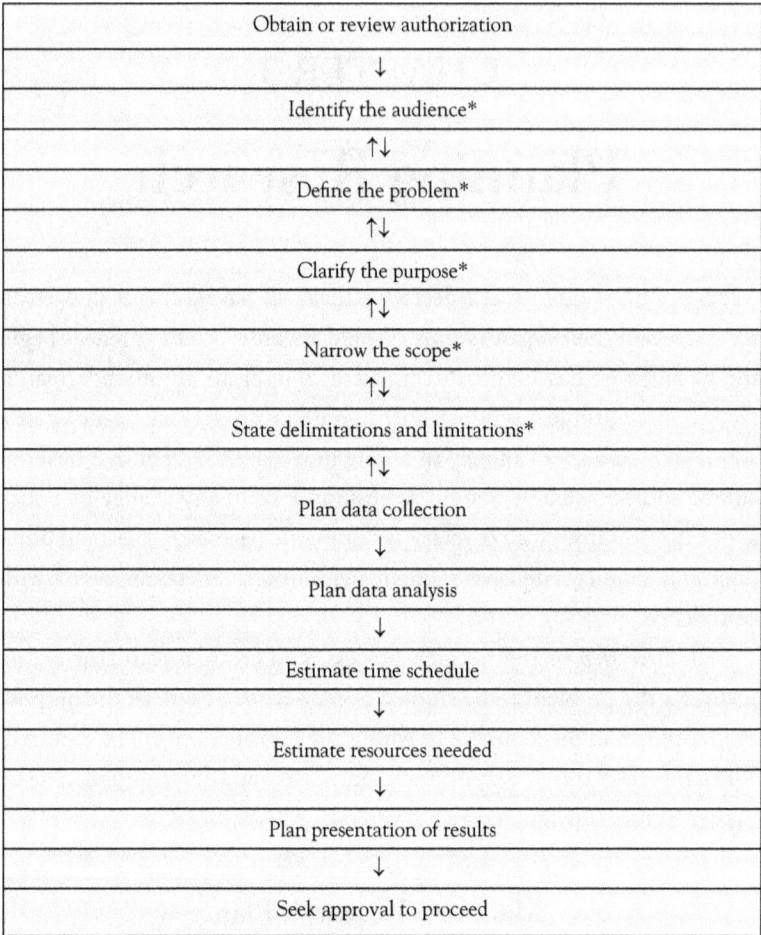

Figure 3.1 A 12-Part Research Plan

Notes: *Two-way arrows suggest that a reiterative approach to these parts of the research plan may improve its overall quality.

Obtain or Review Authorization

When a project requires extensive research, you must be sure that you are authorized to spend time or money on the project. In some situations, your job description will require that you prepare specific reports; then you need no additional authorization to initiate a research plan for that report. But you may also discover the need to analyze a unique problem related to your work; then part of your plan is to be sure you are authorized to do the research. In addition, your manager may ask you to work on a special project; your research plan must then include a review of the request to demonstrate that you understand what the manager wants you to do.

Identify the Audience

As when preparing a simple report, you must have a clear understanding of your audience, both primary and secondary. The authorization facts may tell you who will receive your research results, or you may need to determine who they will be. When you initiate a research plan, decide whom you want to influence with the report. When asked to work on a project, clarify who is—and is not—to have access to the information.

Assume, for example, that you must prepare a report investigating feasibility of relocating a grocery store currently located in an economically distressed neighborhood. The intended primary audience would likely be upper-level corporate managers, and releasing information prematurely to anyone not authorized to receive it could result in negative attitudes and behaviors among employees and customers. After deciding to relocate the store, management may ask you to write a report to the employees, who become your primary audience. However, unless employees can be prevented from sharing this information with acquaintances, the potential secondary audience—such as neighborhood leaders, customers, and news media—must also be considered and may influence report content, structure, and tone.

Sometimes you cannot determine the full audience until you have clearly defined the problem. The definition of the problem may provide a clearer view of potential audiences for the report.

Define the Problem

The problem is the central focus of the research. A clear, concise statement of the problem keeps the researcher on target. To conduct business research, you must distinguish between the managerial problem (or symptoms of a problem) and the research problem itself.

The observable phenomena about which a decision must be made make up the managerial problem. Such phenomena are also called the symptoms of the problem. For example, a manager may observe that the office support personnel often are tardy for work; turn in poor-quality work; and complain about eyestrain, wrist strain, and backache. These are all symptoms that something is amiss in the office support system. A manager who considers only one symptom at a time may decide that the resolution to the "problem" is to reprimand tardy employees, give negative work evaluations to employees who do inferior work, or buy new office chairs and wrist rests. But a manager who looks at several symptoms may decide that a deeper problem exists. Perhaps the question that must be addressed is, How can we improve the productivity of our office support staff? That question would become the research problem or research question.

Clarifying the purpose of the report frequently helps the researcher define the problem.

Clarify the Purpose

While the problem defines what is to be investigated, the purpose identifies why the research should be conducted. And when the research is completed, the purpose guides the formulation of recommendations.

In some situations, the problem and purpose are nearly identical. For example, the purpose of investigating ways to improve office productivity would be to improve productivity. When the problem and purpose are similar, they may be stated as the objective of the study. The objective is the overall outcome or goal of a research report.

In other situations, the problem and purpose must be differentiated from one another. Consider Case 3.1, which illustrates how a sound research plan can lead to answers to managerial challenges.

Case 3.1 Assuring the Success of Peaceful Village

As the new administrator of Peaceful Village, a retirement center in operation for three years, you observe several phenomena.

1. The facility has averaged 90% occupancy during the past year, though the goal is 99%.

2. Three new competing facilities have opened during the past year in the Peaceful Village service area.

3. Three months ago, Peaceful Village's dietician and cook took a job with a competing facility. Since then, the residents have complained frequently that the meals served differ considerably from the posted menus. Although the menus sound appetizing, the food is not.

4. Although five potential residents toured the facility during the past month, only one became a resident. That person complained about the intake interview and procedures and almost refused to sign the contract.

5. The head nurse who conducts the intake interviews in the medical office. Personnel who need supplies from the office or must ask the nurse a question frequently interrupt the interviews.

The phenomena suggest a major managerial problem. If the facility continues to operate at less than optimal capacity, it will lose money. If it cannot satisfy its residents, it will likely not operate at full capacity. After some preliminary investigation, the administrator authorizes a study to investigate ways to attract and retain residents. That investigation is the research problem. The purpose of such a study is to enable the facility to reach its goal of 99% occupancy.

1. What are some sources of dissatisfaction among residents and would-be residents of Peaceful Village?

2. What are some potential responses that management could take to solve the occupancy problem?

Having defined the problem and purpose of a study, your next step is to identify the scope of your research.

Narrow the Scope

By narrowing the scope of the analysis, you identify the specific factors or elements to be analyzed. A perfect study would investigate all possible aspects of the research question. However, time and money constraints require that you focus your study on the factors most likely to yield relevant data. Preliminary research often leads to the identification of those elements. After identifying the factors, you will concentrate the remainder of your research on those items.

In the Peaceful Village case, the scope could include these factors regarding attracting and retaining residents:

A. Advertising

1. Cost and benefit analysis of current program
2. Analysis of competitors' advertising

B. Intake procedures

1. Work-flow analysis of current procedures
2. Analysis of procedures used in other facilities
3. Residents' evaluation of current procedures

C. Services to residents

1. Food
2. Recreation
3. Entertainment
4. Personal and medical services
5. Maintenance of private rooms
6. Maintenance of common areas

Notice that the scope remains focused on the problem of attracting and retaining residents. It does not, for example, include looking at alternative uses for the building and grounds. That factor is outside the scope of this research problem.

State Delimitations and Limitations

Two concepts—delimitations and limitations—relate to narrowing the project's scope. Delimitations are additional boundaries or restrictions that you place on the study. For example, in the Peaceful Village study, a decision to interview only current residents is a delimitation. Interviewing only current residents prevents you from knowing why former residents left and why people who toured your facility did not become residents. Failure to acquire that information may seriously limit the validity of your conclusions. If, however, you do not delimit your study in this way, you may find it extremely difficult and costly to locate those nonresidents. Practical constraints may make the delimitation necessary.

Limitations are potential shortcomings or inadequacies of the study. Some limitations arise from circumstances beyond your control, such as being allowed only one month for the study or finding only a small fraction of current residents willing to be interviewed.

Delimitations and limitations are not required in all research plans, though effective planners include those items when they are relevant. Stating delimitations tends to clarify and refine the scope; stating limitations demonstrates that the researcher understands and is willing to acknowledge the inherent weaknesses of the proposed study.

Having carefully defined the problem, purpose, and scope of the study, you are now ready to plan how you will collect relevant data.

Plan Data Collection

The first step in data collection is to identify potential sources. Researchers use two kinds of data: primary and secondary. Information that has been collected and published by others is secondary data. Books, magazines, journals, and corporate annual reports found in public or private libraries are examples of secondary data sources. Many traditional secondary sources are now available through Internet services and online databases. Primary data consist of information collected at its origin. People (customers, employees, suppliers) and company files are major sources of primary data used in business research. (Please note that "data" is the plural form of "datum." Always refer to data with a plural pronoun and accompany the word with a plural verb.)

The scope of the research problem directs the selection of data sources. To ensure the validity of the data, sources must be chosen for their relevance, not their convenience. Two questions should guide you as you determine possible sources for research data:

1. What kinds of information do I need to answer the research question?
2. Should I use primary or secondary data sources—or both—to obtain that information?

Data Need

The research question, divided into appropriate elements or factors of analysis, must direct your search for data. After you have defined the research question clearly and have narrowed the scope, you must focus your attention on finding data directly related to those factors.

Keeping the scope of analysis in mind will assist your efforts to be both efficient and effective as a researcher. You will be efficient because you will target your data search toward the sources most likely to yield meaningful information rather than wasting time looking at unrelated data. You will be effective because you will be able to judge all data in terms of their relevance to the research problem and will not be tempted to include interesting but irrelevant data.

Figure 3.2 shows how the research question guides the selection of information sources. For each element in the scope, specific kinds of data and specific data sources must be identified. Note that more than one kind of data and more than one data source may be required to analyze an element adequately.

Primary Versus Secondary Data

Effective business researchers use both primary and secondary data to solve business problems. Primary data are data acquired at their sources through observation, experimentation, interviews, question-naire surveys, and searches through company records. Secondary data consist of information that others have accumulated and made available through books, magazines, journals, and other published documents. Other important sources of secondary data include print and journals and fact books, information made available on commercial databases (such as Business Source Premier/EBSCO and LexisNexis) and on the World Wide Web, and resources stored electronically on microfilm or fiche or CD ROM.

Elements (scope)	Data needed	Potential sources
Projected demand for skilled heating, ventilation, and air conditioning (HVAC) technicians	a. Sizes of projects under contract by major regional contractors	a. Regional contractors
	b. Projects to be bid and contracted for during next three years	b. State economic development boards
Projected supply of skilled technicians	a. Demographics of crews currently hired by major HVAC contractors in the northwest	a. Regional HVAC contractors; state employment services
	b. Projected graduates from technical schools in the northwest for next three years	b. Registrars and placement officers of technical schools
Air Waves recruitment and employment practices	a. Methods currently used to locate skilled HVAC technicians	a. Air Waves director of human resources
	b. Air Waves employment practices that attract technicians to Air Waves	b. Members of current Air Waves crews
	c. Air Waves employment practices that deter technicians from working for Air Waves	c. Former Air Waves technicians

Research problem: To project market conditions for skilled construction labor in the northwest United States during the next three years.

Research purpose: To ensure that Air Waves has an adequate supply of labor to fulfill installation contracts.

Figure 3.2 Determining Data Sources

Some researchers mistakenly consider primary data to be better than secondary data. They assume that information "straight from the source" is better information than secondhand data. Others prefer to use primary data because they are stimulated by that data collection process and feel restricted when they must sit in a library searching through documents or in front of a computer monitor using search engines to find secondary information. In contrast, some researchers—equally mistakenly—suspect the accuracy of primary data. They recognize that people can deliberately distort self-reported information, and researchers can make incorrect observations or lead people to report what the researcher wants to record. In addition, some researchers may feel uncomfortable with the primary data collection process but enjoy the sense of discovery that comes from searching out well-documented information in secondary sources.

Neither attitude can produce consistently effective research reports. When you recognize a problem and the need for research, you should first consult secondary sources. Secondary sources often provide information to help define the problem more clearly and to identify elements that should be investigated. After narrowing the scope of the analysis, you must determine whether primary or secondary sources will best answer each element of the problem, as was demonstrated in Figure 3.2. When the problem you are investigating is unique to your organization, primary data may be the only usable information. But if adequate secondary data are available, you should use them instead of relying solely on the time-consuming process of collecting from primary sources.

For team research projects, team members should work together to identify possible data sources. If the research requires the use of primary data, one or two members of the team might be responsible for designing the questionnaires or interview guides. In any case, all members should participate in a critical review of those instruments before they are used.

Plan Data Analysis

Data analysis is the process by which researchers find meaning in the many facts and figures they have accumulated. Both quantitative and qualitative analysis procedures are used in business research. Quantitative analysis involves the use of statistics to derive meaning from numerical data. Qualitative analysis is the use of logical thought processes to discover relationships and meaning in data. Take note that even before you collect data, you must decide how you will analyze them.

Although some people consider quantitative analysis to be the more objective form of analysis, that method also has a subjective component. Selection of statistical procedures and interpretation of the computations rest on subjective judgments. In both quantitative and qualitative analysis, the researcher must avoid faulty reasoning. For example, a researcher could make a hasty generalization about the interrupted intake interview referred to in the Peaceful Village case. In a hasty generalization, the researcher concludes that something that was true in one instance is true in all cases. If the observed instance was an unusual situation resulting from unexpected events on that day, the researcher would be in error to design a study to determine how to improve intake interviews. The interview situation also could be a symptom of a larger management problem, such as the lack of standard procedures for several aspects of the operation.

When a team conducts business research, team members often work independently during the data collection phase, each person collecting and interpreting data for the segment of the study for which he or she is responsible. After the data are collected and analyzed, the group should again work together, discussing the data, evaluating its adequacy, and agreeing on its interpretation.

The manager must know when the project will be completed. Therefore, the proposal should include a realistic estimate of time required for the work.

Estimate Time Schedule

The purpose of a time schedule is twofold. It ensures the manager that you have considered carefully the time required and are making a commitment to keep to that schedule. It also serves as a checklist for people working on the project to remind them of obligations at various stages. The terms of a research proposal often become part of a formal contract; some contracts include penalties if the project is not completed on time or bonuses if completed ahead of schedule.

An effective time schedule includes target dates for completion of various segments of the project as well as a projected date for presentation of the results. It may also include dates on which you will make interim or progress reports. When given a deadline for a project, an effective method for developing a time schedule is to work backward from that date and allocate the maximum length of time that can be devoted to each phase of the project. If no deadline has been given, you may work forward from the date of the proposal and project the amount of time required for each phase.

Estimate Resources Needed

Research always requires time; in addition, some research requires special equipment or supplies. In all cases, human resources are needed. Before approving a project, a manager must know how much of the company's resources the project will consume. A research plan should include realistic estimates of the costs of necessary labor (researchers and assistants), supplies, equipment, travel, and so on. The manager can then evaluate the potential benefits against the projected costs of the research.

In many companies, the accounting department has developed standard costs to apply when employees prepare research proposals. For example, when you prepare a proposal, you will often follow standard cost procedures for determining the value of the time that you and your associates will spend on a project. However, it is your responsibility to make a realistic estimate of the kinds of personnel and the number of hours a project will require. You can usually obtain costs for equipment and supplies from vendors, but it is your responsibility to assess realistically the quantities of such materials that will be required. You can get reasonably accurate estimates of costs for airfare and lodging from a travel agent or online services provided by airlines and hotels. Company policy may require that you use a company vehicle for land travel. If you are permitted to use your own vehicle, apply your employer's standard mileage allowance or the Internal Revenue Service's allowance.

Plan Presentation of Results

Research has no value until the results have been communicated. A complete research plan indicates how the findings, conclusions, and recommendations will be disseminated—that is, the nature of the report.

Since research deals with a nonroutine problem, a relatively rich medium must be chosen. That medium is usually a carefully designed, comprehensive written report, perhaps supplemented by an oral presentation.

A tentative outline for the written report may be included in the research plan as evidence that the researcher has thought the project through to its completion.

Seek Approval to Proceed

By now you can probably appreciate that one more item must be included in a research plan: a request for approval. Since research addresses a non-routine problem and may consume substantial resources, the researchers and managers must agree on all items in the plan. Even when authorized to prepare the plan, effective researchers do not assume that it is automatically approved. They specifically request feedback and approval. That request opens the door for clarification, possible modification, and approval of the plan. On approval, the researcher can work confidently, knowing that carrying out the plan will contribute to both individual and organizational goals.

To obtain approval, most researchers write the research plan and present it in a formal document called a research or project proposal. The proposal may also be presented orally so that managers can ask questions immediately, clarify any ambiguities, or request changes before giving their approval.

Preparing a Research Proposal

The objective of a business proposal is to persuade another person or persons to do something that the proposer thinks will be beneficial for the organization and its stakeholders. In the case of a research proposal, the objective is to persuade the recipient to authorize the time and money required to carry out a significant research project.

The persuasiveness of the proposal will depend on your ability to show that you understand the problem and are capable of conducting the study. Additional persuasive elements are honest, realistic estimates of time and resources needed for the project and evidence that you have considered how you will present your results. Therefore, a research proposal is a formal version of your research plan.

Proposal Content

As you prepare a research proposal, use the 12 parts of the research plan shown in Figure 3.1 as a guide. Include all parts that are relevant to the proposed investigation. The situation may justify omission of certain parts. For example, stating delimitations or limitations is not necessary if the scope of the project is already stated very narrowly and no obvious limitations are foreseen.

In contrast, you may want to add specific information to increase the persuasiveness and thoroughness of your proposal. For example, the decision to narrow the scope—that is, include some elements and exclude others—implies a judgment that one route of analysis will lead to better results than another. Such a decision is an ethical judgment. Discussing a research problem with a group of colleagues who can judge the work impartially may help you identify the best set of factors to include in the scope. Then include a summary of that discussion in your proposal. Thus, you show the readers you thought through the problem, and you enable them to follow your reasoning.

Regarding data collection, if primary data are to be used in the research, the researcher and the person who authorizes the research have an ethical obligation to protect the confidentiality of the data and the safety of human and nonhuman subjects. In your proposal, explain the specific techniques you will use to protect confidentiality, safety, or both.

The request for approval is more than a request for authorization of funds. Do you have (or can you acquire) the skills needed to carry out the research as proposed? Conversely, the person who gives approval has an ethical responsibility to evaluate the quality of the proposed research, its value to the organization, and the competence of those who will conduct the research. For that reason, include the qualifications of the person or person who will conduct the study to demonstrate competence to fulfill the proposal. Information of this type usually appears in an appendix with a reference to it in the proposal's request for approval section.

The order in which the parts are presented must contribute to the reader's understanding of what you plan to investigate. The presentation sequence should also lead the reader to appreciate the significance of the research. Since a research proposal is a complex document, structural devices such as headings, enumerations, and columns can be used advantageously, as Figure 3.3 illustrates.

SC state ports authority

Memo

To	Bryant T. Joseph, VP, Terminal Development
From	Melvin L Barbara, VP, Government Relations
Date	01/12/2017
Subject	Citizens' Attitudes toward Cruise Traffic

Background and Authorization

Recent letters to the editor in the *Charleston News and Courier* have indicated mixed attitudes about the docking of cruise ships at Union Pier in the Port of Charleston. For approximately 25 years, the Port of Charleston has been the site of one to three ship departures and arrivals per week. Currently this port serves as a home port and port of call for Carnival Cruise Lines as well as a port of call for other cruise lines. Home porting and port-of-call stops generally do not occur on the same days, except when emergencies, weather conditions, or other nautical events necessitate such multiple dockings. Although some merchants appreciate the increased business associated with the cruise dockings, other merchants and many local residents complain that the increased pedestrian and auto traffic distract from the traditional charm of Charleston. Discussions have been underway to move the cruise port to a different location along the Charleston Harbor waterfront in an attempt to alleviate some of the negative aspects of the departure and arrival of cruise ships.

At our management meeting on January 7 we discussed the need to determine objectively how the citizens of Charleston feel about the effects of cruise dockings in the Port of Charleston. We decided it was necessary to know more about those attitudes before launching a major study of the feasibility to relocate the cruise port. You asked me to design a study to explore those feelings.

Statement of the Problem

The objective of the study is to determine Charlestonians' perceptions of the economic and social impact of cruise dockings in the Port of Charleston and the possible relocation of the cruise terminal.

Purpose of the Study

The purpose of this study is to assess the business and social climate in which the Ports Authority will operate if it continues with plans to relocate the cruise terminal. Knowledge of that climate will help the Authority develop operational and communication strategies relative to the potential relocation.

Scope of Analysis

Three factors will be studied:

1. What business impacts do the Charleston's downtown residents and merchants perceive to be related to the arrival and departure of cruise ships?
2. What personal and community impacts do Charleston's downtown residents and merchants perceive to be related to the arrival and departure of cruise ships?
3. What knowledge of and attitudes toward relocation of the cruise port are evidenced by Charleston's downtown residents and merchants?

Definitions

For purposes of this study, *residents* is used to designate persons living in the Ansonborough section of Charleston. The term *merchants* includes all commercial and professional units within the designated geographical area.

Delimitations

Because cruise passengers primarily frequent the area between the Charleston Harbor and King Street, the sample for this study will be drawn from merchants and residents in an area bounded by East Bay St. on the east, Broad St. on the south, King St. on the west, and Calhoun St. on the north. The sample of residents will be drawn from the Ansonborough district, which is located within those street boundaries.

The study period will be the months of June and August, confined to two days following the departure of a homeport ship and two days following the arrival and departure of a port-of-call ship. Ships will be selected from published cruise schedules, with ships departing at least three days from one another.

Limitations

The data collected will not represent attitudes of the business community or residents outside the downtown area, some of whom may also be affected by the cruise business. However, since the downtown community absorbs the major impact of the presence of cruise ships, the attitudes of that community can best direct decisions related to relocating the cruise port.

Since the data will be collected during the summer cruise season, the attitudes expressed may differ from attitudes expressed during an earlier or later cruise season. Nonetheless, the responses should be representative of attitudes developed during a peak tourist season in Charleston.

Methodology

This study will be based solely on primary data gathered by questionnaires completed by members of the target populations.

The sample. All merchants and residents within the defined geographical area will be invited to participate in the study.

Data collection. The data will be collected in two ways:

1. A letter will be mailed to all merchants inviting them to log onto a specified website on specified dates and complete an electronic questionnaire. The dates will be based on the docking of selected ships.
2. An invitation to attend a town-hall meeting will be mailed to all residential addresses in the Ansonborough district. The meetings will be scheduled to correspond to dockings of selected ships. At each meeting, the purpose of the study will be explained, attendees will be permitted to ask questions, and they will be asked to complete the questionnaire before leaving the meeting.

Data analysis. My staff will code the data obtained from the questionnaires and enter them into a statistical program. Summary statistics will be computed and interpreted.

Time Required

I propose the following schedule:

March	Design, test, and revise questionnaires; test data analysis program
April	Prepare letters to be sent to merchants and residents
May 1–15	Prepare and distribute a series of three news releases (newspaper, radio, and television) to inform the community about the upcoming survey and encourage participation
May 15–30	Mail letters to merchants and half of Ansonborough residential addresses

June 1–5	Send reminder to attend town-hall meeting
June 12 and 13	Conduct town-hall meetings following June 1 departure of Carnival cruise ship
June 15 and 16	Conduct town-hall meetings following June 15 port-of-call docking of Carnival cruise ship
June 17–July 30	Begin data entry and analysis regarding June dockings
August 1–5	Mail letters to remaining half of Ansonborough residents; mail reminders to merchants
August 14 and 15	Conduct town-hall meetings following August 13 departure of Carnival cruise ship
August 23 and 24	Conduct town-hall meetings following August 22 port-of-call docking of Carnival cruise ship
September 1–15	Complete data entry and analysis
September 20	Distribute completed written report to management committee
September 22	Discuss report with management during regular meeting

Resources Needed

All research will be conducted by staff of the Government Affairs Division as part of our normal duties. We will use approximately 100 employee hours to prepare the data collection instruments, enter and analyze the data, and prepare the final report. We anticipate spending approximately 24 employee hours conducting the town-hall meetings. Standard cost allocations for respective grades will be applied.

In addition, the project will incur direct costs for printing, supplies, postage, and town-hall meetings. The total project budget is $5,750, as follows:

Staff Labor	$3,750
Printing and supplies	750
Postage	750
Meeting expenses	500
Total	$5,750

Presentation of Results

I will present our findings, conclusions, and recommendations to the management committee in a formal written report prior to our September 20 management meeting and will be prepared to discuss the report at that meeting.

Request for Approval

Approval of this proposal by January 20 will permit the Government Affairs division to work this project into our schedule and adhere to the proposed schedule given in this proposal. If you have any questions in the meantime, please e-mail me (bryant.joseph@scspa.com).

Figure 3.3 Research Proposal*

Notes: *Figures discussing research related to the cruise port in Charleston, South Carolina, are based on actual events, circa 2011. However, all names, data, and dates used in the figures are fictional.

Proposal Formats

While Figure 3.3 shows a proposal in memo format, that proposal could also be presented in manuscript format, including a title page and transmittal message. In this instance, the transmittal message would be in memo format, because the proposal is going from one individual to another in the same organization.

Figures 3.4 through 3.6 show a proposal prepared in manuscript format. In this case, the transmittal message is in business letter format, because the proposal is going from one organization (NKG Design) to another (SC State Ports Authority). Whether letters, manuscripts, or memos, proposals usually will be converted to PDF (to preserve the formatting) and sent as e-mail attachments.

The Feasibility of Relocating

the Cruise Port at Union Pier

Charleston, SC

A Proposal

Submitted to

Bryant T. Joseph, VP, Terminal Operations

South Carolina State Ports Authority

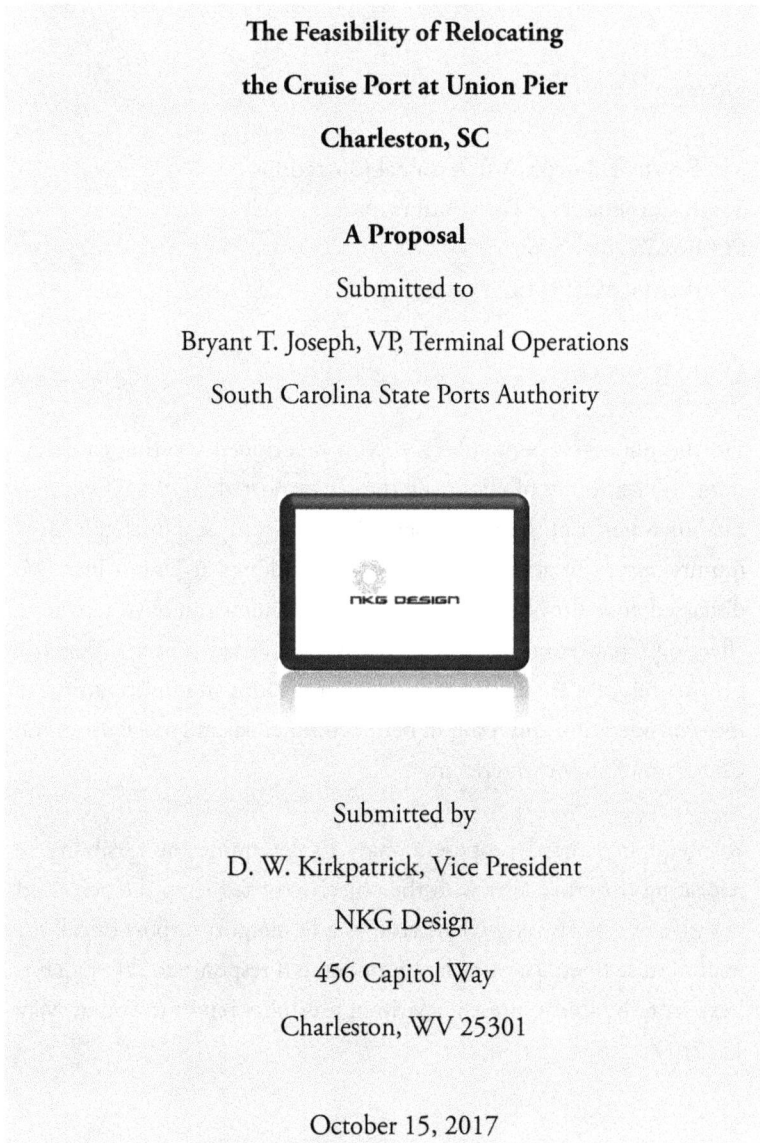

Submitted by

D. W. Kirkpatrick, Vice President

NKG Design

456 Capitol Way

Charleston, WV 25301

October 15, 2017

Figure 3.4 Research Proposal Title Page

Designing Tomorrow's Communities Today
456 Capitol Way, Charleston WV 25301
Tel: 888.888.8888 Fax: 888.123.4567

October 15, 2017

Mr. Bryant T. Joseph, VP, Terminal Operations
South Carolina State Ports Authority
PO Box 22288
Charleston, SC 29413

Dear Mr. Bryant

On the phone on September 28, you mentioned wanting to determine the feasibility of relocating the cruise port along the Charleston Harbor waterfront. You said that you had already conducted a community survey of attitudes about cruise dockings at Union Pier. We discussed your firm belief that the cruise business can have a positive effect on Charleston's economy. You also expressed concerns that any plan to relocate the cruise terminal must take community attitudes into consideration and result in better commercial and social use of the Charleston Harbor waterfront.

You requested that I propose a study to determine the feasibility of relocating the cruise pier with the objective of reducing the perceived negative effects of using Charleston as a home port or port of call for major cruise lines. The attached proposal is a response to that request. I expect to be able to present a written feasibility report to you by May 15, 2017.

Approval of this proposal by November 15 will permit NKG Design to begin and end on schedule. Of course, I'll gladly answer any questions you send my way (cell phone 888-321-6543).

Sincerely

D. W. Kirkpatrick

D. W. Kirkpatrick, Vice President

Figure 3.5 Research Proposal Transmittal Message

A Proposal:

The Feasibility of Relocating the Cruise Port at Union Pier, Charleston, South Carolina

A study conducted by the South Carolina Ports Authority in Summer 2016 revealed mixed attitudes about the economic and social benefits of cruise dockings in the Port of Charleston. A sizable majority of merchants approved of the dockings and reported that their businesses had benefited from the cruise traffic. In contrast, a majority of downtown residents expressed considerable dissatisfaction with the increased pedestrian and motor traffic in the area as well as the abrasive announcements made from the ships and pier directed to cruise passengers during embarkation and debarkation.

The Ports Authority is tentatively considering a relocation of the cruise port to an area slightly north of its current Union Pier location. Tentative plans call for redirecting motor traffic along the waterfront and increasing public space to provide greater waterfront access to Charlestonians and tourists. The Authority hopes that relocating the cruise port may reduce some of the dissatisfaction expressed by downtown residents and ultimately make a large portion of the waterfront a major community asset. In general, downtown merchants were knowledgeable about the potential economic and social impact of relocating the cruise port; however, residents had incorrect or inadequate information about that impact.

Statement of the Problem

The focus of this study will be to determine the feasibility of relocating the cruise port to an area slightly north of its current Union Pier location, including related changes in traffic flows and waterfront usage. Three factors will be analyzed:

1. Optimal location for a new cruise terminal
2. Infrastructure and traffic needs
3. Public use of Charleston's historic waterfront

Purpose of the Study

The purpose of the study is to generate a concept plan for the Union Pier waterfront that will enable the Ports Authority to serve the contemporary needs of the cruise industry while retaining the traditional ambiance of historic Charleston.

Methodology

Both primary and secondary data will be used in the study. Secondary data will be obtained by a review of current security standards related to cruise embarkations and debarkations, records of current use of port facilities both as a cruise terminal and a shipping terminal, Charleston County tax assessor's data, and current zoning regulations.

Primary data will be obtained by way of a photographic survey of the entire area under study, followed by engineering and economic studies of pedestrian and vehicular traffic, infrastructure needed to service the port area satisfactorily, and alternative uses for the Port of Charleston waterfront.

To conduct this study, NKG Design will assign a team of licensed engineers and economic analysts who will employ standard engineering and economic analysis techniques.

Time Required

This study will be completed within six months of contract signing. An interim report will be provided at the end of three months.

Final Report

A comprehensive written and fully illustrated concept plan will be presented to the Ports Authority. This plan will be accompanied by all engineering and financial studies conducted to formulate the plan.

Qualifications to Conduct Study

NKG Design has a track record of compiling successful concept plans for major urban waterfront renewal projects in North America and Europe. Examples of those projects are available at our website: www. nkgdesign.com.

Cost

NKG Design will conduct this study for a turnkey figure of $200,000, with a penalty of $2,000 per day for failure to deliver the final product within six months of contract signing.

Figure 3.6 Research Proposal in Manuscript Form

This entire manuscript proposal could have been prepared as a business letter. In that case, the background information in the transmittal message (Figure 3.5) would appear at the beginning of the letter, and the request for approval would appear at the end.

Proposal Templates

Models of proposals for business services abound on the Web. Even your word processing software may include a proposal template. Use templates prudently. While they are helpful for giving your proposals a professional appearance, no template can replace the kind of careful planning advocated in this chapter. So adapt any template, such as the research proposal template available at PandaDoc (www.pandadoc.com), to your specific needs.

Proposal Approval

The person who received a proposal from you may send you an e-mail, letter, or memo indicating approval and stating what the next step(s) will be, leading to a formal contract. You could save time and effort, though, by using electronic signature technology to, in effect, turn your proposal into a signed contract.

For relatively short, simple proposals involving comparatively few resources, you might insert spaces for an electronic signature, or e-signature, at the end of the proposal itself. In high-stakes situations, you might include a formal contract—sanctioned by your organization's legal counsel—in an appendix, with spaces for one or more e-signatures. To do this, you would upload your proposal file to an online signing service and mark or tag it where you want signatures to appear.[1] The signing service would then e-mail this marked-up file to whomever you specify. A receiver of the tagged file could sign it using the options available. For example:

- Type his or her name and select from various fonts to make the name look like an authentic signature.
- Draw the signature using a computer mouse or touchpad.
- Take a photo on a smartphone of the signature and upload it.
- Draw the signature with a finger on a mobile device that has the e-sign application installed.

The numerous online e-signing services vary in ease of use, features, pricing, and how they prove the validity of e-signatures over time. Therefore, the choice of an e-signing service requires study. A few reputable examples include the following:[2]

- Adobe Document Cloud (formerly EchoSign) (acrobat.adobe.com)
- DocuSign (www.docusign.com)
- RightSignature (rightsignature.com)
- Sertifi (www.sertifi.com).

A research proposal—a formal description of a research plan—is meant to persuade its recipient to approve a research project and commit the time and funds necessary to do it. E-signing is a means of expediting proposals. Approving a proposal by e-signing it makes it a legally binding contract, just as would a handwritten signature.

Summary

A research plan will guide you toward completion of effective research. Content and context determine the formality of the plan. Include these 12 steps when planning a complex research project.

12-Step Checklist for a Research Plan

☐ Obtain or review authorization. Are you approved to spend time, money or both on the research?

☐ Identify the audience. Who will receive your research results—both the primary and secondary audiences?

☐ Define the research problem. Go beyond the managerial problem and its symptoms to the bigger picture. Put the problem in question form.

☐ Clarify the purpose of the research. What do you hope to accomplish by doing the study? If you can, separate the purpose from the problem.

☐ Narrow the scope of the problem. You may not be able to study all parts of the research problem; so ask, which parts will lead me to useful facts?

☐ State your delimitations and the limitations. What boundaries are you drawing between what you will and will not study? Could any practical limits on your research lower its applicability to the problem? Explain.

☐ Plan for data collection. What kinds of information will you need to answer the research question? Should you use primary data (collected from records or people or both), secondary data (collected and published by others), or both?

☐ Plan for data analysis. Does the context call for qualitative or quantitative data? If the latter, then determine what statistical test to apply to the data you will collect.

☐ Estimate the time schedule. Plan backward from the due date, setting interim dates for completing each phase of the research.

☐ Estimate the resources needed. Include realistic estimates of equipment, labor, supplies, travel, and other costs.

☐ Plan the presentation of results. What will be the nature of your research report? What rich communication medium will you use to make your findings, conclusions, and recommendations known?

☐ Ask for approval to proceed. Present your research plan in person, in writing, or both and seek feedback. In most instances, you will want a contractual agreement before continuing with the project.

A research or project proposal is a formal, persuasive version of a research plan, delivered orally or in writing. It is an opportunity to show your understanding of the research problem and indicate your ability to conduct the proposed study.

To add to a proposal's persuasiveness, arrange it attractively in business letter, manuscript, or memo format. Until you master the 12 steps of research planning, avoid the use of proposal templates. Electronic signature services are becoming commonplace in business. Approving a proposal by e-signing it makes it a legally binding contract.

Notes

Chapter 1

1. Wilson (2016).
2. Alred, Brusaw, and Oliu (2006, 265–69).
3. Lewis, Simons, and Fennig (2016).
4. Weiss (2005, 4–7).
5. Weiss (2005, 7).
6. Weiss (2005, 25).
7. Thrush (2001, 293).
8. Weiss (2005, 40).
9. Weiss (2005, 7).
10. Weiss (2005, 7).
11. Richardson (n.d.).
12. Weiss (2005, 53).
13. Richardson (n.d.).
14. Martin (2001, 20–33).
15. Richardson (n.d.).
16. Weiss (2005, 72).
17. Weiss (2005, 73, 74).
18. Weiss (2005, 48).
19. Weinstein (2013).
20. Christensen (n.d.).
21. Badaracco and Rosenbaum (n.d.).

Chapter 2

1. Farace and MacDonald (1974). In this classic study, Farace and MacDonald identified three purposes of organizational communication: production, innovation, and maintenance. Some readers may not readily associate the term maintenance with the idea of maintaining employee morale. Therefore, in this book, the term goodwill is used to cover that concept.
2. Lengel and Daft (1988).
3. Lengel and Daft (1988).
4. Einstein (n.d.).
5. Lengel and Daft (1988).
6. Sabin (2010).

7. These guides adapted from two sources: Mitchell (n.d.); Peters and Griffiths (n.d.).
8. *Chicago Manual of Style* (2010).
9. Tuckman (1965). For abstracts of Tuckman's findings, see Smith (n.d.). Also, Free Management Books (n.d.).

Chapter 3

1. Null (n.d.).
2. McFarland (n.d.).

References

Alred, G.J., C.T. Brusaw, and W.E. Oliu. 2009. *Handbook of Technical Writing.* 9th ed. New York City: Bedford/St Martin's.

Badaracco, J., and D. Rosenbaum. May 24, 2006. "Making the Best 'Right' Decision." CIO. www.cio.com/article/2446373/careers-staffing/making-the-best--right--decision.html (accessed January 11, 2016).

The Chicago Manual of Style. 2010. 16th ed. Chicago, IL: University of Chicago Press.

Christensen, D.S. 2010. "Four Questions for Analyzing the Right-Versus-Right Dilemmas of Managers." *Journal of Business Case Studies* 6, no. 3. www.cluteinstitute.com/ojs/index.php/JBCS/article/viewFile/877/861 (accessed January 11, 2016).

Einstein, M. n.d. "Is E-mail a Rich or a Lean Media [sic]?" www.emailoverloadsolutions.com (accessed March 11, 2016).

Farace, R.V., and D. MacDonald. 1974. "New Directions in the Study of Organizational Communication." *Personnel Psychology* 27, pp. 1–15. http://onlinelibrary.wiley.com/doi/10.1111/j.1744-6570.1974.tb02060.x/abstract?systemMessage=Wiley+Online+Library+will+be+unavailable+on+Saturday+14th+May+11%3A00-14%3A00+BST+%2F+06%3A00-09%3A00+EDT+%2F+18%3A00-21%3A00+SGT+for+essential+maintenance.Apologies+for+the+inconvenience (accessed February 29, 2016).

Free Management Books. n.d. "Bruce Tuckman's 'Stages for a Group'." www.free-management-ebooks.com/index.htm (accessed March 2, 2016).

Lengel, R.H., and R.L. Daft. 1988. "The Selection of Communication Media as an Executive Skill." *The Academy of Management Executive* 2, pp. 225–32. www.jstor.org/stable/4164833?seq=1#page_scan_tab_contents (accessed February 29, 2016).

Lewis, M.P., G.F. Simons, and C.D. Fennig. n.d. "Ethnologue: Languages of the World." www.ethnologue.com (accessed February 5, 2016).

Martin, P. 2001. *Word Watcher's Handbook.* iUniverse.

McFarland, T. n.d. "10 Electronic Signature Options and Why You Should Use Them." Small Business Trends. www.smallbiztrends.com (accessed March 18, 2016).

Mitchell, O. n.d. "18 Tips on How to Conduct an Engaging Webinar." Speaking About Presenting. www.speakingaboutpresenting.com (accessed March 2, 2016).

Null, C. n.d. "E-signatures: The Complete Guide to Paperless Signing." PC World. www.pcworld.com (accessed March 18, 2016).

Peters, C., and K. Griffiths. n.d. "10 Steps for Planning a Successful Webinar." TechSoup. www.techsoup.org (accessed March 4, 2016).

Richardson, P. n.d. "When in Rome: 5 Surefire Tips for Communicating Over Borders." Priscilla Richardson: Business Writing for Success. www. priscillarichardsonva.com/business-writing/communicating-over-borders/ (accessed January 23, 2016).

Sabin, W.A. 2010. *The Gregg Reference Manual*. 11th ed. New York City: McGraw Hill Education.

Smith, M.K. "Bruce W Tuckman—Forming, Storming, Norming, and Performing in Groups." InFed: The Encyclopedia of Informal Education. infed.org/mobi (accessed March 2, 2016).

Thrush, E.A. August 2001. "A Study of Plain English Vocabulary and International Audiences." *Technical Communication* 48, no. 3, pp. 289–96. www.aviationenglishclasses.com/libary_contents/PlainEnglish.pdf (accessed January 22, 2016).

Tuckman, B.W. 1965. "Developmental Sequence in Small Groups." *Psychological Bulletin* 63, pp. 384–89. http://openvce.net/sites/default/files/ Tuckman1965DevelopmentalSequence.pdf (accessed March 2, 2016).

Weinstein, B. August 1, 2013 "The Five Questions." The Ethics Guy. www. theethicsguy.com.

Weiss, E.H. 2005. *The Elements of International English Style*. Armonk, NY: M.E. Sharpe.

Wilson, B. n.d. "Digital Miter-Gauge Setup." *Wood Magazine*. www. woodmagazine.com/woodworking-plans/jigs/digital-miter-gauge-setup/ (accessed January 19, 2016).

Index

OTHER TITLES IN OUR CORPORATE COMMUNICATION COLLECTION

Debbie DuFrene, Stephen F. Austin State University, Editor

- *SPeak Performance: Using the Power of Metaphors to Communicate Vision, Motivate People, and Lead Your Organization to Success* by Jim Walz
- *Today's Business Communication: A How-To Guide for the Modern Professional* by Jason L. Snyder and Robert Forbus
- *Communication Beyond Boundaries* by Payal Mehra
- *Managerial Communication* by Reginald L. Bell and Jeanette S. Martin
- *Writing for the Workplace: Business Communication for Professionals* by Janet Mizrahi
- *Managing Virtual Teams, Second Edition* by Debbie D. DuFrene and Carol M. Lehman
- *The Language of Success: The Confidence and Ability to Say What You Mean and Mean What You Say in Business and Life* by Kim Wilkerson and Alan Weiss
- *Writing Online: A Guide to Effective Digital Communication at Work* by Erika Darics
- *Get Along, Get It Done, Get Ahead: Interpersonal Communication in the Diverse Workplace* by Geraldine E. Hynes
- *Communication for Consultants* by Rita R. Owens

Announcing the Business Expert Press Digital Library

Concise e-books business students need for classroom and research

This book can also be purchased in an e-book collection by your library as

- a one-time purchase,
- that is owned forever,
- allows for simultaneous readers,
- has no restrictions on printing, and
- can be downloaded as PDFs from within the library community.

Our digital library collections are a great solution to beat the rising cost of textbooks. E-books can be loaded into their course management systems or onto students' e-book readers.
The **Business Expert Press** digital libraries are very affordable, with no obligation to buy in future years. For more information, please visit **www.businessexpertpress.com/librarians**. To set up a trial in the United States, please email **sales@businessexpertpress.com**.

www.ingramcontent.com/pod-product-compliance
Lightning Source LLC
Chambersburg PA
CBHW071905200326
41519CB00016B/4509